HAUNTED LEHIGH VALLEY

KENNETH BIDDLE

4880 Lower Valley Road, Atglen, Pennsylvania 19310

Other Schiffer Books on Related Subjects
Pennsylvania's Adams County Ghosts, 978-0-7643-3123-7, $14.99
Haunted Gettsburg, 978-0-7643-3310-1, $19.99
Franklin County Ghosts, 978-0-7643-3257-9, $14.99
Ghosts of Hershey and Vicinity, 978-0-7643-3285-2, $14.99

Schiffer Books are available at special discounts for bulk purchases for sales promotions or premiums. Special editions, including personalized covers, corporate imprints, and excerpts can be created in large quantities for special needs. For more information contact the publisher:

Published by Schiffer Publishing Ltd.
4880 Lower Valley Road
Atglen, PA 19310
Phone: (610) 593-1777; Fax: (610) 593-2002
E-mail: Info@schifferbooks.com

For the largest selection of fine reference books on this and related subjects, please visit our web site at:
www.schifferbooks.com
We are always looking for people to write books on new and related subjects. If you have an idea for a book please contact us at the above address.

This book may be purchased from the publisher. Include $5.00 for shipping. Please try your bookstore first. You may write for a free catalog.

In Europe, Schiffer books are distributed by
Bushwood Books
6 Marksbury Ave.
Kew Gardens
Surrey TW9 4JF England
Phone: 44 (0) 20 8392 8585; Fax: 44 (0) 20 8392 9876
E-mail: info@bushwoodbooks.co.uk
Website: www.bushwoodbooks.co.uk

Copyright © 2010 by Kenneth Biddle
*Unless noted, all photos are the property of the author.
Library of Congress Control Number: 2009933418

All rights reserved. No part of this work may be reproduced or used in any form or by any means—graphic, electronic, or mechanical, including photocopying or information storage and retrieval systems—without written permission from the publisher.
The scanning, uploading and distribution of this book or any part thereof via the Internet or via any other means without the permission of the publisher is illegal and punishable by law. Please purchase only authorized editions and do not participate in or encourage the electronic piracy of copyrighted materials.
"Schiffer," "Schiffer Publishing Ltd. & Design," and the "Design of pen and ink well" are registered trademarks of Schiffer Publishing Ltd.

Designed by Stephanie Daugherty
Type set in Eraser/NewsGoth BT/Fleurons
ISBN: 978-0-7643-3389-7
Printed in the United States of America

DEDICATION

This book is dedicated to YOU, the reader. Without you, the interest in the paranormal would simply fade away. From the bottom of my steadily beating heart, I thank you.

ACKNOWLEDGMENTS

Special Thanks To...

🌿 Dinah Roseberry — For giving me the chance to do this, as well as having the patience to deal with me!

🌿 My wife, Donna — For putting up with my sudden day trips to the Lehigh Valley.

🌿 Diana, Mike, Irene, Patty, Jeff, Steve, and all current and former members of PIRA — You have all, in some way, contributed to this book.

🌿 Greg and his team from the Eastern Pennsylvania Paranormal Investigation — For inviting me along on their investigations.

🌿 Rick Bugera and his team from the Berks Lehigh Paranormal Association — For allowing me to sit in on their open investigation.

🌿 Finally, to everyone who shared their story with me and now with you...

THANK YOU!

CONTENTS

FOREWORD

I absolutely love ghost stories. Since before I can remember, I have found great excitement in hearing spooky tales of lost souls that still wander the earth. Seriously, what is more intriguing — *more fascinating* — than a good ghost story?

From a young age, I have read everything I could get my hands on having to do with the subject of ghosts. This was long before the term "Paranormal Investigation" became a household name to the majority of us. Back then, ghosts stories were the reason I would stay awake all night, hoping that the "magic" of my covers would protect me from the wicked things that would certainly burst forth from my closet door. As luck would have it, I survived my nightmares to read even more stories of ghosts and hauntings.

As I grew older, my love for all things supernatural also grew. I joined a local paranormal group in Philadelphia and started going out on "ghost hunts." The adventures I had with those people led me to forming my own team of investigators, taking my research and investigation skills even further than before.

My "Field of Study" fell into the realm of photographic analysis. I took the time to do the research necessary to figure out how many of these photographic anomalies were created — by natural occurrences, simple mistakes, or even...deliberate fraud (yes, there are more than a few people out there who crave attention so much that they need to make "evidence"). This led to the writing of my third book, *Orbs or Dust? A Practical Guide to False Positives*, which covered a great deal of the way false evidence of the paranormal is obtained.

However, the first book I did was called *PIRA Ghost Stories: Our Gettysburg Experience*. It was a collection of stories experienced by the investigators on my team. It seemed right, since Gettysburg, Pennsylvania is a special place for us. Most of my team travel there at least once a year. I've even filmed a documentary, as well as two movies in Gettysburg, so it holds a special place in my heart.

After another book detailing our investigative techniques (*A Guide to Paranormal Investigation*), a few of my team members began working on another book about ghost stories. This one was about the ghost stories that really got us into the paranormal and those that have kept us interested. Although we haven't released it yet, it will give the reader some insight into what keeps us going out at night (or during the day), looking for the unknown.

And now, we come to the book you are now holding. This was a project that was born of a conversation that took place in, of all places…Gettysburg. I was at an annual ghost convention, operating a vendor table. It just so happens that next to me, at a vendor table of her own, was Dinah of Schiffer Publishing. As we spoke, she mentioned that they were looking for someone to gather stories in the Allentown/Bethlehem area of Pennsylvania…and she asked if I was interested.

After a few emails and a phone call or two, I accepted the challenge. And let me tell you, it was definitely a challenge! Although the people I spoke with were nice, it was hard to find the few that would open up to me, telling me about their experiences. I sent out emails, posted on message boards, and contacted other groups in the area — with no response. I was stuck. Then one day, I finally received an email back from someone! Kristina Taylor, of Wydnor Hall Inn, was interested in telling me her story…more on that later.

After visiting Kristina and her husband Charles, I found myself once again stuck for stories. I had a few of my own, which I planned on including, but nothing "new." I was looking for stories no one had heard of, instead of retelling the same stories over and over again. I finally came to the conclusion that the "Old School" way was, and still is, the best way to gain the stories I was looking for.

Old School = Walk and Talk, baby.

Simply put, I started traveling to sites that might be haunted, could be haunted, or just looked like they *should* be haunted by the spirits of the dead. Sometimes I wandered around back roads for hours, with nothing more than a few scenic photographs. Other times, I met the right person who was more than happy to relate a story to a friendly face…rather than an impersonal email. The "ball" had finally started rolling!

My weekend adventures soon took me outside the boundaries of just Allentown and Bethlehem, to include places all around the Lehigh Valley and the Poconos. I was going wherever the fates would lead me. Some of these sites you may know, but I'm sure there will be others that will be new to you.

In any case, the purpose of this book is to entertain you with stories of what happens when our side meets up with the *other side*. As you'll find out, this book is not simply a collection of stories I've gathered from local residents of the Lehigh Valley. Since I've had the opportunity to investigate more than half of these locations, I have included excerpts from the PIRA case files. I find this way of storytelling to be enjoyable, since you're not only getting what has happened in the past, but also some first hand accounts from actual investigations.

I hope you enjoy the stories and keep the thrill of adventure alive.

Sincerely,
Kenny Biddle

Kenneth Biddle, Your Humble Author

INTRODUCTION

The Lehigh Valley, prior to the European settlement, was a beautiful land belonging to the Lenni Lenape Indians. They occupied areas throughout much of New Jersey, New York, and Pennsylvania, maintaining an agricultural and hunter-gatherer type of society. Their success as a society allowed them to establish approximately eighty settlements throughout much of what is now known as the New York metro area. It was in 1524 when several Lenape Indians, traveling in canoes, met their first European explorer; Giovanni da Verrazzano made the first contact with the Lenape Indians as he entered what we today call the New York Harbor.

The majority of settlers in the Lehigh Valley area were from various groups of Germans, with many originating from Palatinate, which is a region in southwestern Germany. The Valley drew these immigrants here because of the dense forests and mountainous regions, which looked much like their homeland. The descendents of these early settlers became what we now know as the Pennsylvania Dutch (which several sources insist are not "Dutch," but German).

In the beginning, most of the interaction between the Lenni Lenape Indians and European settlers came in the form of trade. European-made goods, such as metal farming tools, were exchanged for Beaver Pelts (skins/fur). However, the demand for these pelts almost brought the beaver population to near extinction in this area. With the source of the pelts exhausted, the Dutch and European settlers took their trade business elsewhere (mostly to upstate New York). In 1634, the Susquehannock Indians waged war on the Lenape, over the issue of trade with the Dutch settlers of Manhattan. The Lenape were beaten, and coupled with the loss of their fur trading opportunity, the Lenni Lenape population fell into decline.

The Lehigh Valley, as we know it today, got its start in September 1737 with what is known as the Walking Treaty (also known as the Walking Purchase). It was an agreement struck between the Penn family, who were the proprietors of Pennsylvania after the passing of William Penn, and the Lenape Indians. According to several sources, the colonial administrators had claimed they were in possession of a deed, dating back to the 1680s, in which the Lenni Lenape tribe had promised to sell a portion of their land to the European settlers. This "portion" was to begin at the junction of the Lehigh and Delaware rivers (modern-day Wrightstown, Pa) and extended *"as far as a man could walk in a day and a half."*

To this day, the treaty is still disputed. At best, it is believed that the treaty was an unsigned document and never formally approved. On the flip side, many believe it was simply a forged document in order to gain ownership over land that, in reality, was already sold. *What? Already sold?* Yes, it seems that the agents of the Penn family had already sold off larges sections of the Lehigh Valley and were desperate to clear out the Lenape Indians for the European settlers. However, during this time, the Lenape Indians, led by Chief Lappawinsoe, had believed the treaty to be valid. William Penn had built a strong reputation with the native tribes of Pennsylvania, always insisting in dealing fairly with the native tribes. Unfortunately for the Lenape, old Billy had been gone for nineteen years (William Penn died July 30, 1718 at the age of 73) and his descendents did not adhere to their ancestor's morality. This was only the beginning of the "land swindle."

The Provincial Secretary, Mr. James Logan, was a smart man and had planned ahead. Although the treaty stated "as far west as a man could WALK in a day and a half," he had the foresight (and some would say dishonesty) in hiring the three fastest *runners* of the colony. So, on September 19, 1737, three men — James Yeates, Solomon Jennings, and Edward Marshall — set out on the "walk"...running as fast and as far as they could, stopping only to sleep (and I'm sure to catch their breath). You can imagine how intense this task was; it was the 1700s, a large land acquisition was hanging in the balance, and the whole colony focused on how well you do, which no doubt would be reflected in your standing within the community. Edward Marshall was the only one to have completed the day and a half "walk" and actually reached the area of Jim Thorpe, approximately seventy miles from their starting point. Not a bad "walk," when the average walking speed is between two or three miles per hour! (That modern-day statistic is based on even ground, not the valleys, mountains, and unsettled land of the Lehigh Valley in the 1700s!)

Although Chief Lappawinsoe and the Lenape Indians felt they had been cheated, they didn't think they could do anything more than agree to the treaty. The Lenape people continued to fight the treaty, but without any positive action. Eventually, they moved (or more likely were "driven") to the Wyoming and Shamokin Valleys, and then eventually further west into the Ohio area.

Soon, farming villages began to spring up all over the Lehigh Valley. An interesting fact I "discovered" on a Lehigh County website told of how these villages began. Surprisingly, instead of towns building up around a church, they usually developed around a Tavern (these were certainly my kind of people), which usually had a General Store connected to it. During the course of development, when these villages became large enough to warrant a name for itself, they were most often named after the current owner of the original tavern (most of the names were given between the 1820s and 1830s).

During the Revolutionary War, after the Battle of Trenton on December 26, 1776, General Washington had brought captured Hessian soldiers to Allentown. At the time, there were crude prisons located in the area of where Gordon Street crosses the Jordon Creek. The Hessian prisoners were confined here, as were many more prisoners over the course of the war. According to reports, this was one of the most secure places to hold prisoners, with no reported escapes. In 1777, the only church in the city of Allentown had been transformed into a hospital, in order to care for American soldiers. In September 1777, the Liberty Bell had been moved from Philadelphia to Allentown, in expectation of a British attack on Philadelphia. The Bell was taken to Zion's Reformed Church located in the center of Allentown. It was hidden under the floorboards, along with several other Philadelphia bells. Officials feared that the British would melt down the captured bells and cast them into cannons.

The Lehigh Valley then went through its share of ups and downs. The year 1829 saw the completion of the Lehigh Canal, which allowed timber and coal to be floated down to Philadelphia. Business was going good...and then tragedy struck. First came the Panic of 1837, which was followed by a five-year depression. A flood in 1841 destroyed the majority of the buildings, both homes and businesses, along the canal. In 1848, two vengeful workers started a barn fire that would grow to engulf the entire area of central Allentown. However, there was light at the end of the tunnel. The year of 1855 saw the rebuilding of Allentown, as well as the completion of the Lehigh Valley Railroad. Furnaces and Mills were popping up across the land, and quarries were supplying zinc, iron, and slate.

The Lehigh Valley was doing well. Even through more floods, the Panic of 1873, some epidemics of Yellow Fever and Influenza, and not to mention the Civil War, the Lehigh Valley still thrived in its industrial growth, adding silk and the manufacturing of furniture to its offerings. In fact, the Civil War actually helped to boost the industries within the Lehigh Valley, which supplied much needed materials to the Union Army.

Today, the Lehigh Valley still serves as a major center of industrial manufacturing and boasts being one of the larger areas for warehouses and distribution centers on the East Coast. The mountains and forests, small towns, and winding roads make the Valley a beautiful place to live and visit. Driving through its small towns takes you back in time a bit...not too far, but just enough to see how life was before the age of the Internet. However, there is also a side of the Lehigh Valley that will send chills down your spine. Some say that the Valley is...*haunted*!

In the pages that follow, we'll delve into all manner of places that claim to have uninvited guests — from private homes and businesses, to cemeteries and bridges. What I'll be sharing with you are the stories of your fellow Lehigh Valley neighbors, stories that tell of strange sightings and all those things that go bump in the night. I invite you to grab a snack, get comfy, and read on... the adventure awaits you.

BETHLEHEM

WYDNOR HALL INN

When I began this project, I had a case of "Tunnel Vision." I thought I would be able to get the majority of my stories and research done on the Internet. Instead, I found that many of the places I contacted (or attempted to contact) still required a more "hands-on" approach to gathering information.

However, there was one site that returned one of the hundred or so emails I sent out — Wydnor Hall Inn. Innkeeper Kristina Taylor wrote back in her email, *"We do have a pipe smoking, tweed jacketed gentleman who visited with one of our guests. Please let me know if this is of interest."*

I made arrangements to visit with Kristina and her husband, Charles, at Wydnor Hall Inn, to get the scoop on this pipe-smoking spirit. As I followed the directions I had, I found the charming home at the southern portion of Bethlehem. I parked out front, got out, and stood there for a few moments to take in the view. The house really had a charming look to it, and honestly, "Charming" is not a word I use often. I took a few photographs outside and walked up to knock on the door.

I was greeted by Kristina, who immediately set about to make sure I was comfortable. We settled down in the Sitting Room, and after some formality, I explained what I was doing with this book. Kristina listened

Wydnor Hall Inn provides a quiet get-away...with a few ghosts!

patiently and questioned me on several topics, and then began to tell me a little bit about the history of the house — and, of course, about the ghosts.

Prior to the Taylors' ownership, the house was a private home on a much larger property for the better part of the nineteenth century. The house stayed within the Wydnor family, passing down from generation to generation. Over time, parcels of land had been sold off and a man named Bowman had an interest in developing the land, although his plan was never fully realized. Bowman's son had taken over, and it's agreed that under the son's leadership, the property began to decline. In 1963, the property was finally sold at a Sheriff's Sale to a man by the name of Louie Long, a local attorney. The house was converted into apartments and, from the description of how they were run, it was doomed. Tenants were told to simply pay the rent and to leave the owner alone (not a statement of confidence by any means). From that point on, the tenants pretty much did whatever they wanted. Maintenance was not a priority to anyone. By the owners' own statement, this site had become "the shame of the neighborhood that no one wanted to go near."

Wydnor Hall, as Kristina and Charles Taylor found it in 1986. *Photo courtesy of Kristina Taylor.*

Kristina had driven by many times and, although the place was in terrible shape, she saw the "diamond in the rough." As she recalls, one day she drove her husband past and told him, "Look at that, there is just one gorgeous house there." He just looked at it and said, "Well, that's a DUMP!" It was only a few weeks later that this "dump" went up for sale. Kristina and Charles decided to take a look at the place and eventually purchased the property a little later in 1986. The house was still in a state of major disrepair, but the new owners didn't give up. It took over two years to fully restore the building, but the finished product is truly worth the effort. The house is beautiful and it would seem ... *haunted*.

The first stories of ghosts came from former tenants that stopped by. During the restoration of the house, former residents would pop in to see how the house was coming along, and to tell the new owners how good a job they were doing. The former residents would also ask, "Oh, and have you seen the ghost?"

The ghost they were referring to was based on the story of a little girl who had drowned in the Black River Creek many years ago. Whether she was a member of the Wydnor family remains a mystery, for I have not been able to find any record of a young girl drowning here. However, this little girl has apparently chosen to spend eternity within the walls of the Wydnor Hall Inn. One woman, who had lived in the former apartments,

The ghost of a little girl is seen running down this first floor hallway.

traced the path she had witnessed the little girl walking. According to her story (and demonstration), the little girl passed through Kristina's office and into the kitchen area. Kristina admits that neither she nor her husband have ever seen the little girl for themselves.

From the point of view of someone who simply loves ghost stories, this alone would be enough to make me want to stay here. On the flip side, as an investigator of these kind of things, I find it fascinating that several people — who had lived at the same location at different times — came back to report the same experience. They all described the girl as being around twelve years old and passing through the walls of the house, walking the same path each time. This type of experience is called a *residual haunting*, in which events play out the same way each time they are witnessed.

After Kristina and Charles took over and began the renovations, they began experiencing *their own* spooky events. On the second and third floors (but mostly on the third floor), Kristina would get the feeling of being watched. There were several times when Kristina thought she saw a face in the doorway of one of the rooms. She describes it as a man's face without features...more of an outline of a face. It didn't seem to bother Kristina at all, as she kept on working in the room after the face disappeared!

Our final story is that of the Pipe Smoking Ghost. This event took place several years ago, and was experienced by the owner's stepdaughter. The Inn was finally completed and open for business. The owners were going to be away for the weekend and had asked their stepdaughter, Courtney, to stay in one of the rooms and "keep an eye" on the guests. Kristina had called to check up on things, and Courtney said, "I just can't wait till you all get back...I have some story to tell you." Here's the story as it was told to the owner:

It was in this doorway that the owner witnessed the outline of a man's face appear.

It was next to this fireplace where the ghost of a man smoking a pipe was seen by a guest.

One of the guests was staying up on the third floor. It was very late, but she simply could not sleep. With nothing better to do, she decided to head down to the Sitting Room and grab a book to read... hoping that this would put her to sleep. As she came down the stairs, she smelled pipe tobacco. This was not a big deal, since there is a case of antique pipes by the front door. However, when the guest entered the Sitting Room, there was already a man in there. He was standing in front of the fireplace, wearing an old-fashioned tweed jacket with leather patches on the elbows. She sat down with a book and began reading. When she looked up, the man smoking the pipe was gone. He never walked out of the room...he apparently just disappeared.

The next morning, the guest asked Courtney if there was another guest staying there that matched the description of the Pipe-Smoking man. Courtney assured the serious-minded guest that no one fitting that description was currently booked at the Inn. Both Courtney and the guest left the Inn that weekend convinced that a ghost had paid the place a visit. The ghost's identity remains a mystery.

CONCLUSION

My visit to Wydnor Hall Inn was a very pleasant one. I thoroughly enjoyed my time with Kristina and Charles Taylor and the stories they shared with me. If you're up for both a weekend getaway and an adventure, I invite you to contact Wydnor Hall Inn and book a room! You never know what you might find…a little girl passing through walls, a face watching you from the doorway, or perhaps a pipe-smoking man by the fireplace. In any case, you're sure to have an interesting weekend!

Contact Information
Wydnor Hall Inn,
3612 Old Philadelphia Pike
Bethlehem PA 18015
Phone: 1-610-867-6851
Toll-free: 1-800-839-0020
Fax: 1-610-866-2062
Innkeepers: Kristina and Charles Taylor

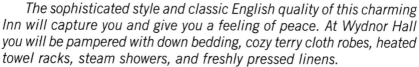

The sophisticated style and classic English quality of this charming Inn will capture you and give you a feeling of peace. At Wydnor Hall you will be pampered with down bedding, cozy terry cloth robes, heated towel racks, steam showers, and freshly pressed linens.

The Inn is equipped with wireless Internet connection, and each room has a television, central air conditioning, and an immaculate private bath. For your breakfast, you will be our guest at the nearby Piccadelly Cafe. So forget about your everyday worries and enter the civilized world of Wydnor Hall.

A FAMILY REUNION

It had been a long time since the sisters had come together, several years in fact. Although two or three may have found time to "hang out," it was almost an impossible feet to get all five sisters, and their children, together in one place at one time.

Finally, after months of planning (and some rescheduling), they were able to agree on a weekend. "Sarah's" house was where everyone would meet (for the purpose of securing this story, the names of those involved, as well as where they are located, must remain secret). It was with high spirits that the sisters, nephews, and nieces finally found themselves together in one place.

The majority of the weekend went by as planned; a trip to the local amusement park, a drive-by of the historic Bethlehem Steel, and a barbecue complete with a struggle over the garden hose, in which everyone became thoroughly soaked! It had been a perfect weekend.

Like with all good things, the end had come for this family reunion. It was Sunday night, and everyone was set to leave for home in the morning. The majority of the cousins were huddled in the Living Room, wrapped up in sleeping bags, fast asleep. It really was more like a camping trip, rather than a weekend stay at Aunt Sarah's.

For some reason or another, "Patty" simply could not sleep. After tossing and turning for the better part of two hours, she decided that a warm glass of milk might help. She tiptoed her way down the stairs and, like making her way through an obstacle course, made it through the sleeping cousins spread throughout the Living Room to the Kitchen.

She was just pouring the warm milk into her mug when she felt *it* — a feeling of being watched. As she described it, the feeling washed over her like a tidal wave. She related this feeling to being in a strange house in the dark. Although she tried to shake it off, the feeling persisted. She began looking around to see if one of the kids had woken due to her moving around in the kitchen and was perhaps standing in the doorway watching what she was doing.

That's when she *saw* them... In the darkness of another doorway (not the one leading back to the Living Room), there appeared two small red eyes. At first, Patty admits, she believed they were simply red lights, perhaps to a video display or one of the kid's toys. What solidified these two red lights as "eyes" was when they blinked.

The realization of what she was looking at hit her like a ton of bricks. She related to me "complete horror filled every inch of my body when I realized that these red lights were eyes staring back at me. The next thing I knew, I was running for the back door and screaming as loud as I could. I didn't stop for my kids, my sisters, or anyone else...I could only run and scream!"

With the first screams out of Patty's mouth, the kids were immediately awake. The sight of Patty essentially running for her life had the kids doing the only thing they could think of — running and screaming as well! In no time at all, thirteen children were all running for the back door screaming, yelling, and crying... and none of them knew why!

Eventually, Sarah and the three other sisters came down (in a hurry) and gathered outside with the rest of the family. When Patty related what she had seen, a close friend and neighbor was called over to check the house. "Charles" and his son came over, armed with shotguns, and checked over the house for intruders, but no one was found inside, and all the doors and windows were still securely locked (except for the back door). In light of the story Patty had related to all of them, the family decided, rather quickly, that camping outside might be fun — and that's what they did (though none of them slept the rest of the night).

During my interview with Patty, she recalled what she had seen that night; she stated that the "eyes" were a little taller than she was. When they blinked, they had moved a little bit, as if the "head" had tilted to the side...perhaps wondering what SHE was looking at. Patty also wanted to assure me that the eyes were floating in the doorway, and not on the far wall. She seems to remember an outline of a head and the body of a man, but also admits she cannot be sure if this was actually something she saw...or if her mind was simply "filling in the blanks" of what she thinks was there. As I watched her telling me this story, I could see the strain in her face as she struggled with these details. She truly believes this entity was a man of about six feet in height.

A search into the history of the house revealed nothing that would give cause to such events. As far as we could find, there had been no deaths in the house or any type of foul play. "Sarah" had known the previous owners and arranged a meeting for me. Although they could not offer any historical information that might explain this experience, they did relate a similar event while they had lived in the house.

Their story took place about twenty-three years ago. Betty and Joe had just moved in and boxes upon boxes of their possessions were piled up throughout the house. After one very long night of unpacking and organizing, Joe had fallen asleep on the couch. He related to me that he awoke — suddenly and fully awake — at about 3 a.m. His instincts told him that something was just not right, and he stood up and began scanning the darkness for signs of something wrong.

It didn't take him long. In the doorway between the Kitchen and the "TV Room" (as Joe called it), was a pair of eyes. He described them as the color of a STOP sign, and they just stared back at him. Like Patty, Joe wasn't too sure as to what these eyes really were. Joe then related the same event, almost word for word, as Patty did; the eyes blinked at him and then they moved as if the head tilted to the side. He added that the tilting was much like a dog when it hears something strange and tilts it's head.

Joe also offers one more tidbit of information; he had the thought that the eyes might be some kind of optical illusion. He moved side-to-side, thinking that if this were a trick, the eyes would disappear and reappear as he moved. This only solidified the fact that the eyes were indeed floating in the space of the doorway, since they remained in the same position…watching him.

Deciding that this "staring contest" had gone on long enough, Joe reached down and grabbed a golf club (luckily, they had not been completely unpacked yet), and then reared back to take on an offensive stance. When he looked back at the doorway, the glowing red eyes were gone. As Joe puts it, "I was beside myself! Did I really see red eyes floating there? I took off, searching the house with my nine iron at the ready. No one was there."

CONCLUSiON

Although I was allowed access to the house in order to find a possible cause for the sighting, I was not allowed to photograph the areas (the owner was concerned, understandably, that identification of the house might cause some unwanted attention). In searching the "scene of the crime," I could not find any way in which the image of two red eyes could be produced in the area where the witnesses claimed to have seen them. The wall beyond the doorway sported a large set of bookshelves in which any lights shined onto them would be distorted by the many books of varying shapes and sizes.

According to the current owners, all the furniture in the house were in the same position as the night of the "Red Eyes." After about an hour of searching, I could find no indication of reflections or alternative sources of light that would explain what both Patty and Joe had witnessed. So far, this event has only happened once during each owner's occupancy, keeping the identity of who the red eyes belong to a mystery.

Please understand that this is a private residence. Out of respect to the owners, both past and present, the location of this house cannot be revealed.

A FORMER FUNERAL HOME

Several years ago, there was a ghost hunting team called the Lehigh Valley Ghost Hunters Society. This author had the pleasure of working with them on several cases, including the one you're about to read. I had gotten into the habit of traveling to the Lehigh Valley area and meeting up with one of the LVGHS' main members, Mr. Joe "One-Eye." The nickname of "One-Eye" came from a profile photo he used to post where he wore an eye-patch.

Whenever we got together, Joe would simply pick me up in his truck and drive us around, searching for haunted and/or interesting locations to explore. On one particular night in January 2002, he picked me up and said we were heading to a private residence that had quite a story. The look on his face said that I was going to have a good time.

Around six o'clock, we arrived at a huge house on a quiet street on the edge of Bethlehem. We grabbed our gear and headed in to meet the owners. We were greeted by a middle-aged gentleman who seemed very pleased to see us. Apparently, he was convinced that the place was haunted and needed someone to tell him he wasn't crazy.

We sat down at the kitchen table and the owner began to relate the history that he and his roommate had uncovered. The structure was originally built as a private home back in 1882. For a time, it was used as a funeral home. The wife of the funeral home operator would occasionally throw tea parties for the community, making the family well known in the area. It eventually became a private home again and then housed a print shop for a few years. At the time of my investigation, there were four gentlemen living in this large Victorian house, and they were hard at work restoring it to its former glory.

After sipping his coffee, our host (for our purposes we'll refer to him as "John") looked at me and said, "I touched the ghost, ya know." Intrigued, I asked him to continue his story. He went on to say that it was a few months ago. His Mother had recently passed away, and John was feeling down, almost depressed, about his personal loss. It was the day of his Mother's wake; he had just finished getting dressed and was heading downstairs.

As he rounded the lower level of the stairway, he saw an older woman standing by the front door, patiently waiting by herself. Thinking that this was perhaps the mother of one of his roommates, he continued down and approached the woman. In a friendly gesture, John neared the woman, asking her, "Can I help you, Ma'am?"

The woman, who had not made eye contact yet, looked up at John now and replied, "Come in. I'm sorry for your loss. There is a prayer service beginning in the back, and refreshments will be served afterwards." This was confusing to John, and he was just about to ask the woman what she meant, when he caught sight of someone moving in another room. He turned to see who it was, but lost sight of the person. As he turned back towards the woman, he reached up and put his hand on her shoulder. As soon as he made contact with her, her image became translucent and disappeared. John was left standing alone, with his arm stretched out.

The next day, the day of his Mother's funeral, he came down the stairs and once again saw the apparition of the woman. This time though, the experience was a bit different. She recited the same phrase, but her image was fuzzy. John described her as "simply not completely in focus." He approached her cautiously, and once again reached out to her. Just like the day before, once he made contact with her, she became translucent. Basically, all the color faded from her image and he could see through her…into the living room beyond. Within seconds, she was gone.

He remembers nothing unusual about the way the woman felt… she was warm, and the clothing felt like real clothing. However, John says he's stumped as to what she was. He admits that the more he had thought about it, the more he was convinced that she was a ghost, rather than a "walking dream." For several months, it was assumed that the woman was the spirit of an employee of the funeral home. However, John wasn't completely satisfied with that explanation.

As I mentioned earlier, the owner had been doing renovations. Due to the demands of placing a house on the Historic Register (another dream of the owner), details of the construction work had to be exactly as it was when the house was built. During their research, it was revealed that the second owner's daughter, "Lizzie," was still alive and living in the local area. John contacted her, and invited Lizzie to share her memories of the architectural details of the house from when she had lived there in the 1930s.

During her visit, Lizzie shared more than her memories of what the place looked like years ago; she shared family memories as well. She then told a little story that shocked John when he heard it. Lizzie mentioned that her mother almost had a breakdown when her father lost his business. With the impending loss of the house only days away, she would sit in the front parlor and sob for hours. Then Lizzie revealed a surprising detail — her mother would keep busy by socializing and holding prayer services in the house. After which, she would serve refreshments to her guests.

This information simply astonished John, who now firmly believes that he not only came face-to-face with Lizzie's mother many years after her death, but that he had also physically touched her as well. It was a truly amazing experience that he assures me he will never forget. Incidentally, during a previous investigation, two EVPs were recorded in the front parlor. The first sounded like a woman crying. The second, an investigator had asked if the spirit would like them to leave. On playback of the recording, a faint but clear "Yes" could be heard.

This was not the only paranormal activity that had gone on in this house. Over the years, the four current owners had been remodeling the house with a dream of turning it into a Bed and Breakfast. During renovations, another woman has been seen moving in and out of the bedrooms on the second floor. One night, while one of the guys was getting ready for bed, he went for the light switch by the door and noticed something in the transom window above the door. When he looked up, he saw a young woman's face staring at him. This kind of freaked him out for two reasons; first, he didn't recognize this woman at all. Second, to be able to look through that window, she had to have been about twelve feet above the floor! He moved to the door and swung it open…only to find an empty hallway.

The identity of this woman is still unknown, even though the current owners have done extensive research. The younger woman has been seen on several other nights, simply walking between the bedrooms. Her actions are described as being similar to a mother checking in on her children at night. She goes from bedroom to bedroom, and seems to lean over something. She's even been seen going through the motions of "tucking" someone in. However, the bed that this apparition sees is not always where the current one is. She's gone through these motions with nothing but air beneath her.

A third ghost—a male figure—likes to walk between the first floor rooms, as well as in the basement. John tells me of a time when they had a contractor out to the house for some repairs. The contractor was working in the basement, which was the former Casket Showroom, when an older man approached him. The old man demanded, "Why are you in my house!" The contractor left in a hurry and refused to return. It is believed, at this time, that this is the spirit of the original owner of the home. Although the man was a successful grocer, he died in the house, of all things…food poisoning.

Just when you think there was enough activity in this house, I have more to tell you! There are sounds of small footsteps on the second floor, as well as a more disturbing audio experience — around 3 a.m. the sound of roller skates can be heard making their way down the second floor hallway, followed by the sickening sound of crashing and tumbling down the main staircase. Among the research John was doing, there was a discovery that a small child had died, accidentally, in the house. No other details were given, but we have a pretty good idea of what kind of accident it was.

Other paranormal activity includes random voices, the front parlor shaking, doorknobs turning, and other "out of place" noises. The activity seems to increase during the daytime hours. The owners have also noticed that activity spiked when the furniture is re-arranged.

After collecting all of this information from the owners, I set off to tour the house. During a previous investigation, Joe "one-eye" had documented some activity at this location, and I was curious about seeing if I could duplicate those results (my first goal is to rule out any natural or artificial causes before considering the supernatural). Although I could not successfully duplicate the events Joe experienced, we were able to document some rather interesting

An investigator is seen next to the piano that exhibited a fluctuating electromagnetic field...even after the main power to the house was turned off.

activity. There seemed to be a strong, fluctuating electromagnetic field around an antique piano that was recently brought into the house. A reading of 3mg (on my EMF meter) was taken from the center of the piano. I should note that the piano was a self-playing model, but was not plugged in (nor had it been in some time). Suddenly, the field died, then came back hitting as high as 4mg on my meter. Even though I could find no natural source for either the high reading or the fluctuations, we had the owner shut off the main power to the house. Interestingly, we still had a reading of 3mg from two EMF meters (from two different manufacturers).

But wait! It gets better...the field actually moved to the center of the room, between Joe and I. Only now the field was jumping between 2mg and 4mg. Joe, who was using a Natural Tri-Field meter, was getting the same results. When the meter was again placed on the piano...nothing. Later on in the night, we found the field again at the piano! We checked for any electrical devices that might be on a cycle, which would cause this kind of fluctuation. We could not find any such source...especially since the main power was still off.

Our small team moved up to the second floor, where again we found an odd electromagnetic field in the front bedroom. This just happens to be over the front parlor room. We were getting a strong field off the bed. Here's the strange part; the field could only be detected from the center of the bed. Using both EMF meters again, we found that once we moved off towards the edges of the bed, the field dropped off sharply. We still had the main power switched off in order to rule out the building's electrical system. Yet, the electromagnetic field remained constant, no matter what we did.

After a bit of discussion, Joe and Mindy (Joe's wife) went down to the first floor while I took reference photos of the entire second floor. While I was writing down some notes about these photos, I caught movement down the hall, by the front bedroom — where we registered the strange electromagnetic field over the bed. As I looked up, it was just in time to see the back part of a figure walk into that room. I only noticed it had black (or dark colored) pants on. Realizing that that did not fit the description of anyone in the house, I called Joe and Mindy up and told them what I saw.

We took some more readings and found that the electromagnetic field now spread over the entire bed. My EMF meter was holding steady at 5mg over the entire surface of this bed, almost as if the entity was lying down on it. Joe was getting the same readings from his tri-field meter. After a few minutes, the field began to fluctuate,

In the center of the bed, this EMF meter held a steady reading of 5mg. The main breaker to the house had been switched off, so there were no power sources nearby.

bouncing between 2mg and 4mg, until it finally held steady at 1.5mg over the bed. I set up for a Q&A session here, using my digital recorder and micro-cassette. However, I had no results after reviewing the recordings.

Ah, but the night was still young! The next paranormal event took place in the front parlor. A tape recorder had been set up in here all night. I decided that I would try an experiment; I closed off the doors to this room and sat by myself. I set the digital recorder on a nearby table and began asking various questions. I was using a low-frequency microphone that was tied into both the recorder and a set of headphones I was wearing. During the session, I asked the question, "Did you use to work here?" I wasn't expecting to hear a response, but I heard a clear and distinct, "Yes, sir." Although it was quick, it was loud and clear. I'll tell you this — it was a bit disturbing to be in the dark by myself (at least certain that I could see no one in the room with me) and hearing a voice come through the headphones. Disturbing yet exciting at the same time.

During another session, the microphone I was using was tapped. Although the lights were off, there was plenty of light from the street to see in the room, and I saw nothing near the end of the microphone. When I say the microphone was tapped, I mean that it sounded like someone slapped the top of the microphone with their hand. The sound was loud and caused me to jump (both from startling me and by how loud it was). No further questions received any answers.

After this last EVP session, we wrapped up for the night. However, I was able to do a follow-up investigation a few weeks later in which one of my team members (Patty A.) attended. We had one event during this follow-up investigation that is worth including here.

We were in the second floor hallway, simply looking around. The main stairs are a winding staircase, with an open middle area. I leaned over the banister and looked down, and was surprised to see a woman standing there, looking back up at me. She was a young girl, perhaps in her early twenties. She had dark hair, pulled back and parted in the middle. Her dress was plain, nothing flattering, lightly colored (blue). Her hands were folded in front of her, like a servant's would be. I looked into her face and saw sadness. She was looking up at me from the second step of the main stairs. I had a strange feeling that I was looking into the past; the whole scene had a look like it was from "a flashback in a movie." The vision lasted a minute or so, and then everything was back to normal.

At the same time, Patty was at the other end of the hall. She looked down to where I was standing, but did not see me. Instead, she saw another man standing in my place at the banister, looking down the stairwell. Patty described him as having a medium build, about 5'7" tall, maybe a little taller, with dark hair. He was wearing a black suit jacket with black pants. Within a few seconds, the vision disappeared and all she saw was me.

CONCLUSION

Since my investigations of this former funeral home, the owners have renovated the house, restoring it to its former glory. The house is a beautiful example of what hard work can accomplish. On that note, the house is also a very private residence in the Lehigh Valley. My apologies go out to all of you, since I cannot reveal the actual location. Sadly, the owners have declined any further investigations from any group, choosing to live peacefully with the spirits. I am still hopeful that we will be allowed to investigate the site in the near future, but we'll have to wait and see.

ALLENTOWN

THE LADY IN THE BLUE DRESS

*L*ocated in the historic district of Allentown, there sits an old graveyard by the name of Union and West End Cemetery. Although it is now one cemetery, it started out as two. The land for Union Cemetery was purchased April 17, 1854 and included eleven acres (for the cost of $2,200). The land for West End Cemetery was purchased some time around 1876, and included nine acres (for the cost of $1,150). The two strips of land were right next to each other, and on May 4, 1895, they were merged into one large cemetery.

Over time, as the cost of maintaining the cemetery went up, funds were quickly running out. During the 1970s and 1980s, the problem of vandalism became a serious issue. In 1997, the funds had finally dried up and, sadly, the cemetery was abandoned. Without the hand of man caring for the property, nature — in the form of high grass and weeds — quickly overtook the cemetery. Unfortunately, the vandals and drug dealers also took to the cemetery for a time. It was during this time that many of the unique statues on the grounds were broken or disfigured. A sad time this was for sure!

However, all hope was not lost! In 1999, some of the local residents got together and formed a brand new Board of Directors. With the help of grants from both the state and private sector, the cemetery has once

The Union and West End Cemetery is located in the heart of Historic Allentown.

again become a place of peace for both the living and those who have passed on to the next life.

In my weekend travels, I had passed this cemetery more than a dozen times. I always had the urge to stop and walk around, but each time I was simply pressed for time with appointments, meetings, and the need to get home for dinner, so I never had a chance to stop. That changed one Sunday afternoon after a conversation with a friend of mine, who happens to be a local ghost hunter.

As our conversations usually go, the topic turned to the paranormal. After our normal discussion and debate about the differences between investigative teams, I mentioned I was collecting stories in the Allentown area. He immediately perked up. "I've got one that I haven't seen published yet. Want to here it?"

"Ah…yeah," I said, with a note of obvious sarcasm in my voice, and out came my little notebook.

He went on to tell me this interesting tale…

This is one of the many unique statues that required repair.

Outside the cemetery, these cannons stand guard.

"Back in the late 1990s, the cemetery was in bad shape. It had been abandoned and it was pretty much forgotten. This was when the first sightings began. People were seeing an older woman, wearing a light blue dress, walking among the headstones. The strange part was that these sightings were not at night, like most other ghost stories, but at dawn. Just before the sun came up, when the sky has that orange color, the Lady in the Blue Dress could be seen slowly making her way from grave to grave. Some said she would walk for a few seconds...and then *fade* away. Other accounts have her trying to clean up, brushing the dirt off of the headstones. According to the stories I've heard, the Lady in Blue is seen the most just after a storm."

The story was good, and I could see that my buddy had more to talk about. So, I asked him to continue...

One of the stories has a man by the name of Ben actually interacting with the ghost...this "Lady in Blue." This experience took place on a Sunday morning in March, though the year is unknown (strange that the month is used in the story, but no one knows the year). However, the story does take note that it took place the morning after a nasty storm.

Our guy Ben had decided to take a walk and thought the cemetery would be a nice, quiet place to take a stroll. As he came

Monuments to both the living and those who have passed on.

around the north corner, he noticed an older woman walking among the graves. Her steps were slow, but seemed to come with a purpose.

The woman was stopping at each headstone, picking off branches, leaves, and other debris left over from the storm. As Ben neared the woman, she raised her head to look at him, seeming to take notice of him, before going back to what she was doing.

Ben noticed that she had a light blue dress on that looked "old-fashioned," but since the woman was older (in her sixties), he figured it was just what the woman was used to wearing. He got within about ten feet of her when she turned and looked at him straight in the eyes.

Something in this woman's eyes caused Ben to stop walking. He simply stood there, staring back at this woman who was staring at him. After what seemed liked hours, the Lady in the Blue Dress smiled, turned, took a few steps to stand in front of another grave, and...*disappeared*. She did not fade away slowly, but was there one second and then gone in a blink of an eye.

Ben suddenly found himself released from whatever "spell" the old woman had over him. He looked around the cemetery, toying with the idea that the old woman had simply run off. However, there was no sign of the Lady in the Blue Dress, or anyone else for that matter. Ben walked over to the headstone where the woman had disappeared and looked down.

"Sarah Simons, Died March 7, 1880, Aged 65 Yrs."

CONCLUSION

Take careful note here, Readers...whether this is the identity of the Lady in the Blue Dress or not, we simply do not know. Who Sarah Simons is still remains a mystery and I haven't found anything in my research that would explain why this woman would stay behind in this life to constantly clean up after a storm. Perhaps she was involved with the original board of directors. Perhaps she was a member of the staff that took care of the grounds. Perhaps her spirit simply has a sense of respect for the land in which she was laid to rest...and comes back once in a while to tidy things up a bit. We may never know.

But if you ever find yourself in the historic district of Allentown after a storm, be sure to stop by the Union and West End Cemetery. Maybe, just maybe, you'll catch a glimpse of an old woman in a light blue dress lovingly cleaning off the headstones. If you're particularly lucky, perhaps Sarah will even acknowledge you with a look...and then disappear right before your eyes.

This cemetery is being restored by local volunteers who work extremely hard to keep the land clear and in good order so that it can remain a place of peace. If, after reading this story, you decide to visit the Union and West End Cemetery, I ask (urge and beg) you to do so with the utmost respect. I ask that you follow the simple Cemetery Guidelines located in the back of this book.

A close up of Sarah Simon's headstone. Is she the spirit that cleans off the headstones after a storm?

Even though I had arrived at the cemetery after a rainstorm, I wasn't lucky enough to catch a glimpse of the Lady in the Blue Dress.

BRUCE THE BUM AND THE OLD IRON BRIDGE

While collecting stories about ghosts, I realized that they came to me in one of three ways. First, the people I approach are more than happy to share their encounters with the other side. Second, I have to go through a lot of hoops in order to gain the trust of people who would otherwise keep quiet and then — *and only then* — I am able to get the story. The final method of obtaining a story, which is my favorite, is when I happen to stumble on to a ghost myself. Such is the case of Bruce the Bum.

It was a Sunday morning and I had nothing to do, which is extremely rare. As I awoke this day, I had decided to take a road trip to Allentown. The weather, however, was not so willing to cooperate. The sky was filled with dark clouds, and the weatherman was claiming it was to rain the entire day. Would this discourage me from the thrill of seeking out new, little-known ghost stories?

Hell, no. Besides, I firmly believe that the weatherman lies, so I grabbed my gear bag, slid into my minivan, hit the local Wawa,

The view of the bridge as I saw it...moments before "Bruce" emerged from a path to the left.

and I was off. I didn't have a solid plan to follow, but there were a few places that had caught my attention while looking over a map. One site in particular, Guth's Covered Bridge, was where I decided to start my adventure.

Unfortunately, there was nothing too exciting about the bridge. I also had to concede that the weatherman was partially right; it was raining off and on throughout the day. I was able to grab some photos, but only because there was very little traffic on the road — there was nowhere to pull over. So, with a car patiently waiting for me to move along, I headed down Iron Bridge Road until I came to, well...the Old Iron Bridge. Built in 1937, the bridge forms a tunnel over the road I was traveling on, as well as over the Jordan Creek.

As I neared the tunnel, a large man came up from the side of the road, from where the creek runs under the bridge, and began walking down the road in my direction. I had stopped my van so I could grab some photographs of the bridge. While I was getting my camera gear out, I was keeping an eye on the man walking closer and closer to me. I had noticed that his clothes fit the classic description of "worn and ragged"; they were torn in places and in a desperate need of a wash. His pants reminded me of the work pants I wore as a mechanic and his shirt was a mix of dirt and grime. He had on a plaid overcoat that had a hole in the bottom left. He walked slowly, and I noticed he was also keeping an eye on me. I had the distinct impression that this guy had taken up residence under the bridge.

He was about fifteen to twenty feet away from me, when I turned to close up my bag and shut the van door. I kept the man in sight through the reflection of my driver's door window. I slid the passenger door shut, fully expecting to see the image of the man reflected in the large glass window I was now staring at. To my complete surprise, I saw nothing but trees, bushes, and grass. In a sudden moment of panic, I spun around, expecting to see the guy almost on top of me. Instead, I found no one. I looked left and right, up and down the road...*the guy was gone*. I looked across the street, into the field, but he wasn't to be found. I ran around the van once, thinking he might have snuck behind the van, but he wasn't there. Anyone watching me would surely have thought I'd lost my sanity.

I stopped and stood in the middle of the street, turning my head back and forth — wondering what to do next and half-hoping the guy would appear again (so I could get a photograph!). After a few

Once through the tunnel, I was able to see where someone could possibly "camp out" for a while.

minutes, an old flatbed truck came down the road. It slowed until the driver was right next to me. An older woman stuck her head out the window and asked, "You OK there, Sweetie?"

I answered, "Yeah, I'm OK," while still looking up and down the two-lane road. The next few words from the woman I came to know as Diane gave me a bit of a shock, as well as the rest of this story. She said, "Son, if I didn't know better, I'd say you just saw a ghost." I looked straight at her, kinda smiled, and related what I had just witnessed.

Diane spoke right up, telling me I had just met "Bruce the Bum."

"Who?"

Right there in the middle of the road, Diane launched into the story. It seems that not long after the Old Iron Bridge was completed, passersby began seeing a man frequently going down and coming up from under the bridge. Eventually, a small camp could be seen on the small piece of land situated under the tunnel. The man came to be known as "Bruce," then ultimately "Bruce the Bum."

Whether this was his real name, no one knows. Nor does anyone know where he came from. Diane doesn't know how long Bruce lived under the bridge since she never met him herself (while alive, that is...keep reading), but she figured it was probably a year or two before he went missing.

The story, according to Diane, goes on to say how a thunderstorm came through the area one night, raising water levels enough to submerge Bruce's camp. Sure enough, the next morning there was not a trace of Bruce, or his camp, left under the bridge. Unfortunately, this also proved to be the last of Bruce, for no one ever saw the "bum" along the road again. Until one day...

Not long after, travelers along Iron Bridge Road would claim to see a man emerge from a path just next to the bridge. As they drove closer, they would report that this man, in ragged and torn clothing, would stare at them until they passed. When the driver would check the mirror, the "bum" was no longer in sight. Some would stop the car, looking all around for this man "who was just there." Others would panic, pressing on the gas to get away from the area as fast as they could.

Diane had her own experience with Bruce, which took place about three years ago. I didn't even have to ask her to share it with me — she got right into her story. Diane started off by saying that she had a hard time convincing family and friends of her encounter with the *other side*.

She was heading down Iron Bridge Road, still about a hundred yards from the tunnel, when she noticed a large man come up from the creek. At first, she thought nothing of it, since it was probably just someone checking out the underside of the bridge. She began to get a little unnerved when the man seemed to lock eyes with her…he didn't even blink! As she passed the man in her truck, she was really freaked out when he then stopped and turned so not to break eye contact.

Diane starts to shake her head at this part in the story. A shiver runs through her as she relates the following details:

> "The man's face was white. Not simply white as in Caucasian, but white as in someone who is sick and the color drains from their face. His eyes were sunk in to his head. It was so freaky, like something from a movie. It still gives me the creeps."

Diane went on to say that she hit the gas, scared that this man was going to hurt her. As she skidded into the tunnel, she looked into her mirror, but there was no sign of the "spooky man." She stopped, regained her courage (also locking the doors), and backed up. Looking down the road, there was no one in sight. She pulled up close to the edge of the road, looking down into the creek area, but still, she saw no sign of anyone.

This was her first encounter with the paranormal — and it certainly left an impression.

I followed the path, finding it quite easy to get under the bridge. It's here that Bruce had set up his small home.

On one side of the bridge, I was able to find a place to park while I investigated the area.

CONCLUSION

In my research, I was unable to come up with any mention of Bruce or any suspected tragedy associated with the bridge. All I can tell you, based on what Diane told me, as well as my own experience, is to show up just after a rain storm. It seems to be the best chance to catch a glimpse of Bruce the Bum.

Where It Is
Old Iron Bridge is on Iron Bridge Road between Lapp Road and North Cedar Crest Boulevard in Allentown. Please be very careful when visiting this site. There really isn't any place to park between Guth's Covered Bridge and Old Iron Bridge. Although, there is a spot to pull over after going through the bridge…

TOPTON

WHITE PALM TAVERN
(FORMERLY THE TOPTON HOUSE)

n July 2003, I was spending a weekend at my in-laws, who live in the Lehigh Valley area. As with any trip here, I was busy exploring the small towns that dot the countryside, stopping at abandoned buildings and even hooking up with local ghost hunting groups to do investigations.

Enter ghost hunter Rick Bugera from the Berks Lehigh Paranormal Association. We had set up a meeting on Saturday to discuss some joint efforts between our two teams. Rick had been bugging me for years to visit a local site by the name of the Topton House, always adding that I'd be amazed at the amount of activity. The BLPA had already done two investigations of the site and was about to do their third investigation on the coming Sunday. Since I finally had the time, I agreed to stop by the restaurant. After my visit to the Topton House, and having the opportunity to speak with the owners, I was invited to come back the following night for the investigation.

During our meeting, Gerry and Francine (the previous owners) told me a little bit about the history of the restaurant. The Topton House Hotel was built in 1859, though other reports have it around 1866. When it was built, it served as a hotel and restaurant for those who

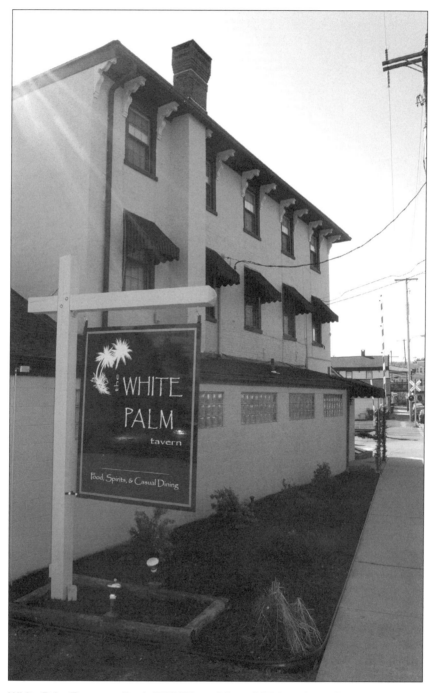

White Palm Tavern — Food, SPIRITS, and Casual Dining...indeed!

The last remnants of a staircase believed to have been part of the Speakeasy that was allegedly run out of the basement.

used and worked on the nearby railroad. In addition to the Dining Room and Bar area, there are several apartments located on the upper floors. There are stories of the hotel being used as a Speakeasy during the days of Prohibition. To further along that rumor...if you go down into the basement of the hotel, the remains of an old, "hidden" staircase can still be found. Honestly, it's not hidden at all, but out in the open

The main dining area of White Palm Tavern. The spirit of a young woman in an old-fashioned dress has been seen walking through this area.

towards the back wall. However, there are modern water pipes and such running just inches above the top step, indicating that it's been quite some time since anyone has used them. There's also an old, wooden beam that was charred from a fire.

Except for a few bumps, the Topton House had been in continuous operation ever since its opening, serving the local community as restaurant, hotel, and bar for over 150 years. Although names will be withheld, several owners of the establishment are known to have passed away during ownership. In addition, there is the report of a possible suicide on the third floor, though no records have ever been found to confirm this.

Over the years, the previous owners (as of 2003) have had several mediums visit, as well as various paranormal teams. Through all the visits and investigations, the owners have come to the conclusion that there are at least three ghosts that continue to "live" in the Topton House Hotel.

The most popular of the spirits is that of a little girl named Emma. Guests and employees have seen Emma throughout the dining room on numerous occasions. A common occurrence in the Topton has been when a guest will comment on how "cute the little girl is"...only to be informed that there are *no* children in the restaurant.

Emma has made herself known in other ways as well. Francine tells me that while she was cleaning up the bar area, the cash register suddenly sprung to life...and rang up a child's drink. The eerie thing is, the register did not have an option for a "child's drink." It should not have been able to perform that function, but Francine suspects that Emma was going to get what she wanted!

Emma has also come through the use of another ghost hunting tool — Electronic Voice Phenomena (EVP). EVP is a process in which the voices (and other noises) of ghosts are captured on audio recordings. During a previous investigation, Jeff (of the North Atlantic Paranormal Association) had taken some video footage of the main Dining Room. In the video, as he approached the Kitchen door, a voice is heard saying, "Hello." After going through the BLPA website, I found many examples of EVPs that are credited to little Emma. Although no one knows why Emma is here or how she came to be

A fellow investigator (Jeff) captured an EVP on his video camera as he walked through this area on his way to the kitchen.

known as "Emma," she continues to make her presence known in the hotel/restaurant.

Another ghost that roams the hotel is that of a Priest. No one seems to know why a priest would "haunt" this hotel, but that's not the most interesting part. Apparently, this particular priest has a definite dislike for the Christmas holiday. During the holiday season, the owners and employees arrived early to prepare for a busy day...only to find decorations ripped down from walls. In different rooms, they have also found Christmas decorations torn to shreds. All of this vandalism is done while the building is locked up for the night. In my interviews and research, I have been unable to find any reason for a priest to be spending his afterlife in this place, much less have a grudge against one of the most popular holidays around.

Our third ghost comes in the form of an elderly man who has been seen tending to a rose garden that no longer exists. The man is seen bending over, going through the motions that a gardener would...only he touches nothing but air. After a few moments, the man simply vanishes. Incidentally, the smell of roses fills the area

The "Rose Garden." It is here that witnesses claim to meet the Ghost of the Gardener tending to the roses that have long since been replaced by the patio.

when this apparition is hard at work in his long-gone garden. On many occasions, it is the scent of roses that predicts an experience with the Phantom Gardner. Guests will catch the scent on their way out to the patio area and see the Gardner hunched down, fully engrossed in his work. When the guests notice the lack of any roses, they usually try to ask the Gardner, "Where are the roses that smell so good?" Without any acknowledgement of those questioning him, the Gardner simply disappears, leaving the guests confused as to what they just experienced.

In addition to the "known" resident ghosts, there are quite a few other strange incidents that go on inside the restaurant. Several employees have reported the scent of roses in the basement, as well as the strong and almost overpowering scent of sulfur at times. To this day, we are still unsure as to the source of the sulfur odor. Servers reported being tripped by unseen feet as they walked through the dining room carrying trays of food and drink. Residents of the hotel also reported being touched by unseen hands, while one resident claimed to have seen a depression appearing at the foot of her bed… as if someone had just sat down on it. After Rick and the BLPA started investigating the building, the owners claim that they've been plagued by electrical problems, as well as frequent phone calls that simply hang up without a word.

Rick Bugera had an experience with the ghost of a young woman. He was sitting at the bar, discussing with the previous owner his plans for the investigation that would be taking place. Rick looked up just as a young woman passed by the doorway into the main dining area. He described the woman as wearing an old-fashioned dress with a bonnet in the back. Actually, he described it as a "Robin Egg Blue" dress. Rick didn't say anything, but got up and looked around the dining area. Some time later, the owner related a story his wife had experienced. Rick was amazed when he was told that she witnessed a woman in an old-fashioned, blue dress. Rick had not said a word about what he had seen only minutes before.

Well, all of these stories got me excited about investigating the hotel myself, so I drove two hours home in order to grab my ghost hunting gear, get some sleep, and drive back the next day. As I was setting up my equipment, one of the current residents of the hotel was kind enough to relate a personal experience to me.

She had been on the stairs, going from the second to the third floor, when she experienced what she describes, in her words, as a kind of "stoppage of time." She said it felt like everything around her went into slow motion. The figure of a man suddenly appeared, coming down

As Rick Bugera (BLPA) sat here with the previous owner, the ghost of a woman in a "Robin Egg" blue dress walked by the doorway you see in the background.

the stairs that she was currently going up (along with her boyfriend). She described him as a solid form and wearing a blue flannel shirt. The area of this figure's head was "fuzzy." She said it looked like when faces are blurred out on TV. The man disappeared just as suddenly as he had appeared. Once he was gone, she became dizzy, needing help from her boyfriend so she would not fall.

After this story, we got started on the investigation. Most of the night was quiet...until I descended into the basement with Rick. The other members of his team were positioned on the second floor of the building. As Rick and I were speaking, we heard the distinct sound of one set of footsteps walking above us, coming to the doorway of the basement and stopping at the top of the steps. Rick called the other team on the radio, asking who had walked into the Dining Room. When we received the reply "No one is over there, everyone is up here in the apartments"...the two of us headed up. As we reached the top of the stairs, no one was found in the area. All the while, we didn't hear any further footsteps of anyone walking away. We were left with the experience of *disembodied footsteps*.

During an investigation, while in the basement, Rick Bugera and I experienced phantom footsteps come to the top of these stairs.

This small hallway behind the bar leads to the basement stairs, and is the path of ghostly footsteps this author experienced first-hand.

This experience was almost an exact repeat of one Rick had during an earlier investigation. He was down in the basement, sitting on a pair of stools with another of his members. Just as it happened while I was present, a set of footsteps walked across the Dining Room floor. The footsteps came to a stop at the basement door and stopped. There were no footsteps ever heard walking away, and when the area was checked, no one was found.

CONCLUSION

2009 Update — The White Palm Tavern

Although I have not been back to Topton House since this investigation, I have kept up on news about it. After appearing on a popular television show about the paranormal (which included Rick Bugera as a guest), the Topton House closed its doors and went up for sale. During a weekend trip in January 2009, I had a chance to visit the site with a friend mine (Greg from Eastern Pennsylvania Paranormal Investigations). The Topton House had reopened under new management; it now goes by the name White Palm Tavern.

Greg and I stopped in, just to see if the interior had been changed. The new owner has done an excellent job updating the decor, giving it a very classy feel. I spoke to two waitresses about any possible ghost stories, but, sadly, they had none to offer. The only thing they could tell me was that there had been a group in here not long ago that checked the place out. They had apparently found some interesting things during the course of their investigation.

As luck would have it, I was able to get in contact with the current owner, Rick Gruber. He agreed to meet with me and give me an update on what's been happening at the Tavern. Since taking over in March 2008, Rick admits that there has not been very much activity. His son actually lives in the apartment upstairs and has frequently been alone in the restaurant while working on the restorations, but he had nothing to report.

However, as Rick and I spoke, little things came out that could be attributed to the ghosts of White Palm Tavern. The first strange experience he recalled centered on the large mirror that used to hang on the wall behind the bar. The owners were in the middle of the renovations, working hard to get the place ready. One day, they watched as the mirror "steamed" up. Rick does admit that it was cold outside and the fogging-effect could have been a result of the weather, but he also admits that it only happened once.

Another interesting experience took place in the kitchen one morning. There is a small, corner shelf back in the kitchen in which several cookbooks are kept. Rick had arrived one morning, to get started on the preparations for the day. As he walked in the back door, he found one of the cookbooks on the floor — a good distance from where the shelf was located. By itself, it really doesn't sound like much

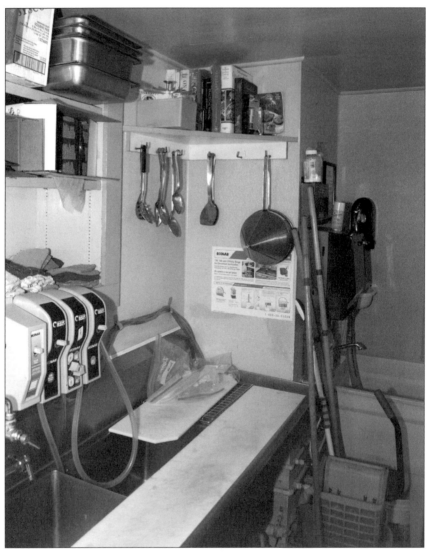

A book from this corner shelf was found on the floor. What's odd is that the book was tucked securely in the middle of everything.

The book, "Practical Baking," doesn't seem like it would easily work itself out and fall to the floor...at least, not without taking a few other things with it.

of a ghostly event, but we must consider the placement of the book: securely tucked in between several other books — actually dead center of seven other books. In addition, it was blocked by a plastic container filled with random items. As you can see from the photos, the book "Practical Baking" is not likely to be the first to simply fall off the shelf. However, the book was found on the floor to the right of where you see the mop and bucket.

Although it doesn't seem to be as active as it was years ago, it's nice to know that the ghosts are still making themselves known. Perhaps the spirits are happy with how the old building turned out and are content to speak up here and there. Or perhaps they're waiting for more investigators to come look for them. There was another team

that conducted an investigation here not long after Rick purchased the property. Although I could not find out who the other team was, Rick did tell me they were able to obtain several EVPs.

 **Contact Information**
The White Palm Tavern
5 Centre Avenue
Topton, PA 19562
Phone: 610-682-5000
Fax: 610-682-5015

4

SAYLORSBURG

LAKE HOUSE HOTEL

The Lake House Hotel started out as a small tavern around the year 1780. The gentlemen who owned the tavern, Charles and Samuel Saylor, were also the founders of the town, which later became known as Saylorsburg. The tavern suffered a fire, but was rebuilt, and renamed, as the Lake House Hotel. Over the course of several years, the owners added on to the building, making it quite a large hotel for its day.

As time went on, the Lake House was used as the Post Office, as well as the local tavern, for the town. As people came through the area, the Lake House Hotel was the place to stay. Local newspapers mentioned how visitors from Philadelphia would come up and stay in the area because the weather was cooler (and much nicer). They even had people from New York coming down and spending vacations in this area.

With the dawn of "technology" and the industrial age in full swing, a (local) man built his business, the Brick Factory, next door to the Lake House. At first, it was only a one-chimney brick factory, but the owner was a smart guy. He brought a man over from England to make a very special type of brick. It wasn't the normal "red" brick that you might be

The Lake House Hotel is a popular "Haunted House" that may have a few "real" ghosts still hanging around.

used to — it was more like a ceramic brick with an enamel coating, making them real shiny. In a short time, this one-stack brick factory turned into a seventeen-acre brick factory.

Around the same time this was going on, large lime deposits were discovered across the street from the Lake House. Blue Ridge Lime Company came in and opened up seven mines. In addition, the railroad came through, grabbing ice from the lakes and transporting it to areas south, such as Philadelphia.

Eventually, the Brick Factory bought the Lake House and used it to house the employees of all three businesses; the Brick Factory, the Limestone Mines, and the Railroad. So, you can imagine that the walls of the old hotel have seen a lot of human drama played out over its more than two hundred years!

In 1919, just before the Great Depression (1929), the Brick Factory fell on hard times. The English gentleman that had the secret (and well guarded) recipe for the special bricks was gone. We're not sure if he passed away, or if he went back to England. Either way, he took the secret recipe with him, and the factory was never able to make the bricks the same way again. As a result, orders decreased because of the lower quality.

With the stock market going all weird, there was a lot of junk bonds that were coming to fruition, but there was no money to cover them.

The Brick Factory and Lake House were victims of these and eventually changed owners. Sadly, the Brick Factory fell silent. All that was now left was the Lime Mines.

Eventually, times settled down and the Lake House was again a place to stay, even hosting weddings and a good twenty years worth of Halloween Balls (which I hear was a big shindig). The hotel again changed hands, becoming an Inn (restaurant) up until the 1970s. It then became an antique shop and, eventually, a small bar, which was located in the basement. Victoria, a friend and fellow paranormalist, said her father-in-law remembered it as a "trouble" bar, where all the vagrants in society would gather together and fights had become a daily event. There is a report that the man who ran the bar was robbed and beaten badly. He was not the same man, mentally, after the beating. His injuries were also pretty severe, and the poor guy died shortly after.

It was a few years later that the Lake House was opened as a "Haunted House" attraction, and ever since, that's what it has been — and that is how I came to know about the site — but more on that later. However, the ghost stories at the Lake House actually started with a

The entrance to the basement bar area...where several people witnessed a shadow figure.

The imposing sight of the Lake House Hotel. For this author, it just seems to scream: "I'm Haunted...Come check me out!"

story published in a book about local ghosts stories in the Poconos area. During the Great Depression, Saylorsburg is mentioned as being the "place to hang yourself." Although the Lake House is never mentioned by name, it somehow became associated with hangings. Since including Lake House Hotel in the book you're now reading, I was contacted by my friend Victoria, who was kind enough to stop by my home and relate much of the history of the Lake House. A dominant story among the locals is that a total of fifteen men have hanged themselves from the front porch of the hotel.

In all the research she has done over the years, she has not been able to find any written evidence that the fifteen hangings actually took place. This certainly does not mean it did not happen, since it could have easily been something the locals would have rather forgotten than to publish for all to see.

There is one story Victoria found that involved a single hanging: a man checked in and was given a second floor room all the way in the back. He simply walked up to his room and hanged himself — no one knew why. In speaking with some of the older folks in the area, it seems that this was a common practice when life got too difficult at home; men would simply check into a hotel somewhere and take their own lives. Sad, really, when you think about it.

Another tidbit from Victoria — she did find a story of a man who got hurt in the mine. It seems it was pretty severe because he was brought over to the Lake House and placed on the porch. A few hours later, this is where he passed away. A common practice for workers who were injured in the mines was to either take you home to your family...or over to the porch of the Lake House, where the poor fellows most likely died (there were no ambulance services back then, let alone decent medical care).

In the present day, Victoria was visiting the Lake House, and at random, snapped a photograph of the front porch. It wasn't until about three months later, while going through these photos, that her oldest child pointed out a guy looking out the window. She described the man as having a really long beard and wearing a miner's outfit.

Victoria has gone back several times in an attempt to duplicate the image in this photograph. She's spoken with the owner and was granted access to the interior, in order to inspect the window. At the present time, she has no explanation for how the image was caught. I've known Victoria for about year and have had the opportunity to work with her

View of the front porch, where workers from the mines and/or brick factory would be brought if badly hurt. Some men took their last breaths here before passing to the other side. It's also rumored that over fifteen men hanged themselves on this porch.

on an investigation where we spent several hours trying to figure out the cause of a photo of another apparition (we eventually debunked the photo). I can say with confidence that she is just as picky as I am when it comes to peeling away the layers of evidence.

For the last few years, as the staff is setting up for the Haunted House, Victoria stops in to say "Hi"...and to catch up on the latest stories. The recent sighting is of a guy, in his twenties, wearing a Hoodie (a sweatshirt with a hood attached). Staff will be in a room setting up, and they'll notice this guy by the doorway. When they walk out into the hall to see who it is, they see the boy walk into a room. When the staffer heads down to the door, they usually find that the door is closed, or they'll walk in the open doorway to find an empty room.

There is also the common problem of missing items within the hotel. Usually, I do not consider "misplaced" items as evidence of paranormal activity. Most of the time, it is a simple a matter of forgetful people. However, this place seems to have an unusually high level of misplacing. One report was of a carpenter putting down a hammer, went off to get something, and then coming back and finding his hammer gone. It was lost for an entire month and later found in different area of the building. Being a mechanic, I know that my tools are my life (and my income). Guys like us do not misplace tools on a job.

Footsteps are another common occurrence at the hotel. During renovations, there were two accounts — by two different people at different times — of people hearing footsteps in the rooms above them, on the second floor. Both individuals had the same reaction; they freaked out and left. During an investigation, Victoria and Rick Bugera (of the BLPA) experienced the same phenomenon. Several members of the investigation had heard footsteps moving around the second floor and then moving to the stairs as they made their way down. Victoria and Rick were standing at the bottom of the stairway at the time, witnessing the entire event...*but never seeing a person attached to the footsteps*.

Finally, my turn to visit arrived. It was November 10, 2007 that I was invited to a public ghost hunt hosted by Rick and his team, Berks Lehigh Paranormal Association. I had contacted Rick with the intention of picking his brain for ghost stories for this book. He said I was in luck, and told me that his group would be the first allowed to investigate the Lake House Hotel, and this might turn out to be a good story for my book. Rick insisted that I attend, so I packed up my gear and off I went. The following is a report of the events that took place that night.

It was through this doorway that the author witnessed a yellow light hovering inside, as well as a shadowy figure moving about.

I arrived a little after 6 p.m. at the old hotel. Although the event was not to start until 7, there were already quite a few people standing around waiting to get in. I walked in and found Rick, who proceeded to introduce me to the rest of his team. After some discussion with various attendees, Rick gathered everyone in the main room and gave a short introduction. He went over some basic rules of the night, explained some of the equipment his team uses, and finally split the crowd into two groups.

My group went to the second floor of the building, which turned out to be completely uneventful. Half the floor had been taken over by the popular "Haunted House," so many of the rooms were blocked off or occupied by tortured mannequins. About halfway through this session, Rick called over the radio, asking for me to come outside. Since nothing was going on, I took my leave and joined him outside in the parking lot...where the night was about to get exciting!

The Shadow Man

Rick and I were talking about various paranormal groups and the "pros and cons" of each when something caught my attention. I had been looking at the door to which we had entered (and just exited) when I saw a light rise up from the right, just inside the doorway. The best description I can give is that it looked like a cheap, dollar store flashlight. The beam was dim and had a slight yellow tint to it. At first, I believed it to be a reflection from a car on the street behind us, but a quick look confirmed that no vehicles were on the road. I moved side-to-side, thinking that perhaps I was catching a streetlight or simply a reflection of something. The light did not waver and remained in the same position, which I finally realized was inside the building.

I asked Rick where the hallway to the right, inside the doorway, went. I had still not mentioned what I was seeing. He said that there were stairs that went down to the basement and then asked me, "Why? You see something, don't you!"

It was at this time that a head and shoulders became visible out of the shadows inside the doorway. As I uttered, "I just watched a light come up and there's a guy standing there," the head and shoulders disappeared and the light, which had been visible the entire time, seemed to turn and drop down...and then it was gone. I related the rest of the experience to Rick and we headed in to see if anyone from the group had broken off and ended up downstairs. We checked in with both teams and found that no one was "missing" or on a bathroom break. We searched the entire basement level and found no one down there. I should note that from what I could see there was only one way down to the basement...and that was the path we had just taken.

During our search, we passed through a small room that was, due to the Halloween Haunted House, set up like a wizard's laboratory. As I entered this room, I immediately felt a heaviness — a pressure on my chest that felt like someone was giving me a bear hug, squeezing my chest to make it hard to breathe. I said nothing at first, wanting to see if the feeling was there after a few minutes. To my disappointment, the feeling was completely gone when I returned a few minutes later. I related my experience to Rick, if only for a notation in my case report.

We continued our search/investigation of the basement...

In the largest room, we found a rather large Halloween prop that included a pond (yes, with real water in it). As we circled this very detailed prop, movement on the other side of the pond caught my attention; a tall, dark figure — *commonly referred to as a Shadow Person* — was standing in the doorway to the adjoining room. Surprised and excited to see this entity twice in one night, I shouted

It was in this room that several people witnessed the tall shadow figure moving past the doorway. In the back, the chair that had appeared in the middle of the hallway.

at Rick, "There he is, over there! There! No, other door! THERE!" The figure moved back behind the wall and out of sight. The two of us rushed over in the "hopeless" hope that the figure would still be there...but alas, it was not.

This time around, I had gotten a good, long (about five seconds worth) look at the figure. He was solid, with absolutely no transparency to him at all. The build of the figure suggested it was male. I asked Rick to stand by the doorway in order to gauge an approximate height; the figure was about six inches taller than Rick, who stands at about 5'11". This put our entity somewhere around 6'4" to 6'6". Yes, he was a tall guy. He had a large build, not skinny and not overweight. There were no other details I could make out. He had no facial features to speak of, nor was any of his clothing identifiable.

It was obvious to both Rick and I that this would be a good time to do some EVP work (Electronic Voice Phenomenon). I brought out my digital recorder and we began taking turns asking questions, allowing a few seconds between each for a possible response. After reviewing the recording the following day, there were no responses found.

We had the feeling that the "show" was over for now, so we decided to head back upstairs and join the rest of the group, who were warming up by the fireplace. I shared my experiences with the rest of the team, who all became eager to visit the basement for themselves. Steve (BLPA member) asked that I show him the areas where I had seen the Shadow Man, so we walked down to the basement. As I went through a re-creation of the initial sighting, we walked down the stairs and headed down the hallway towards the rear section of the basement. I stopped dead in my tracks, for there was a slightly broken chair placed in the middle of this short hallway. I must admit, it took me a little by surprise. Steve noticed the confused look on my face. "I'm guessing that chair wasn't there when you came up?" he simply stated.

While we were down here, Rick and I had walked through this hallway at least four times. The hallway is not very long, nor is it very wide. When the door at the end of the hallway opened, there was barely an inch of clearance between the door and chair. The location of the chair in the center of the hall would have guaranteed that we would have walked into it, or moved it out of the way to get by. It was simply unavoidable where it was at this

This is how we found a chair. Just behind it, there is a door that goes to the second half of the building. Rick and I had walked this hallway several times and had never seen the chair. It appeared from nowhere.

We decided to set the chair in a specific position (later marking the position of the legs) in order to see if it would move again. A video camera was placed on it as well.

time. Steve went to get Rick, to show him what we had found. Once he saw it, his first question was, "Where did that come from?" We had no idea where this chair had actually come from. After snapping some photographs of the location, we moved the chair out of the hallway and marked its position...just in case *it* decided to travel again.

I should note here that the building had no heat, except for the fire the BLPA members had built in the fireplace, and a propane heater. The average temperature throughout the entire structure averaged between 40 and 44 degrees...a chilly night indeed! Although there were times throughout the night when the temperature "felt" like it dropped considerably, the most noticeable drop measured only two degrees. This is not a significant amount, considering the weather and the building's lack of central heat.

The Case of the Ringing Telephone

My next stop of the night was to the fourth floor, where there is an old, crank-style telephone hanging on the wall that reportedly receives phantom calls. BLPA members told me that on at least one occasion, the bell on this ancient communication device had rung...despite the fact that it was not hooked into any telephone line. Like the rest of the group, I was interested in inspecting this device for myself. After a slightly confusing search through another maze of bloodied and disfigured mannequins, I found the telephone.

With the help of an attendee, Chris, who had become my partner throughout the night, we took the telephone off the wall and inspected the "insides." As the photograph shows, there wasn't much. In fact, this "telephone" is nothing more than a prop, rather than an actual antique telephone. The metal ball that represented the striker between the bells (which would cause the "ringing" when someone called) was simply a nail with a balled end driven into the wood. It didn't have the ability to move back and forth, let alone strike either bell. Oh, and it was definitely not hooked into any phone line — it was simply hanging on the wall.

Chris and I settled into this room with six other people and Jen (BLPA member). I placed my digital recorder on a desk and waited. After getting the other groups settled and quiet, we turned the lights out and sat in silence for a few minutes. Without warning, my recorder sounded a "beep" and shut off. I was using an Olympus VN-3100PC, which gave me six hours of "super" high quality and seventy-two hours of low quality recording. There was three hours worth of space left, and the settings were the same as they have been for previous

The author posing with the Phantom Phone, which is said to ring at times. The strange part is, this is nothing more than a prop, and has no way of actually ringing.

As you can see, the Phantom Phone does not have any working parts. If this phone has rung, it certainly didn't do it on its own!

investigations. I could determine no reason for the device shutting off. I hit the RECORD button, the red LED lit up, and placed it back on the desk.

I asked Jen if it would be all right to start asking questions, which she was fine with. I began my usual routine of questions, such as "What is your name?" and "Did you live in this building?" Once again, I found no results when I reviewed the recordings the next day. Although I asked for the spirits to "give us a call," the telephone didn't make a peep. The session ended and everyone headed for the main room, to once again feel the warmth of the fire.

The Shadow Man — Part II

The first two sessions had focused on the second and fourth floors of the hotel. The next two sessions were now going to focus on the third floor and, much to everyone's excitement…the basement. The reasoning behind this schedule was to keep at least one floor between the groups, so not to cause any interference from each other (noises from one team could bleed over to the recordings of another). I joined the group heading to the basement, along with Rick, Darlene (BLPA member), and my unofficial partner, Chris. The majority of the group headed towards the back section, where it was considerably warmer. My group, along with two other women, stayed in the area where I had previously seen the Shadow Man.

With the lights off again, we sat in silence for about five minutes. There are three open doorways into this room, and as vehicles passed by outside, the light from their headlamps would shine through these doorways, slowing illuminating the area, then darkening again. I found myself staring out the middle doorway. I thought I had caught sight of my Shadow Man leaning in from the right side (my point of view) and blocking the incoming light. However, with the amount of darkness surrounding us, I just wasn't sure. I told the rest of the group what I was seeing, but none of them could confirm my sighting.

We decided to begin some EVP work with me asking the questions. I began with my usual routine again, but stopped short since I had gone through these questions once already. I asked, "Could you just step into the doorway?" Rick spoke up, saying, "I just saw that! Did you see that?" Chris, who was on the other side of me, confirmed that he also saw this figure. Excited, I continued… "Can you do that again?" Once again, Rick spoke up, seeing the figure lean in from the open doorway again. By now, everyone in the room had seen this Shadow Man lean in, blocking out the light from outside. Within three minutes, everyone present noted a temperature drop. Even though the infrared temperature gun registered only a two-degree drop, even I had to admit that the difference felt significantly more. The Shadow Man ceased poking his head out and the session ended a few minutes later. The EVP recording did not yield any positive results.

The entire group met up again around the fireplace for a quick break, before swapping locations and heading out again. I really wanted to go back down to the basement and, lucky for me, several members of the next team heading down there approached me and asked if I would join them this time around. So, off I went, with my partner Chris right behind me. This group was considerably larger than the last and everyone packed together in order to get a similar view to what I had in the previous sessions.

I had taken up position in a large doorway, so that I could see both the room where I had been sitting previously and the room (and exact area) where the Shadow Man had been standing. I had caught sight of him, ever so briefly, standing in front of a wall and moving off to my left. Before I could get a word out about this, another attendee stepped next to me, saying he had seen it too…and described the actions of this figure before I had told him. We tried an EVP session, but "Fred" (as I named him for no particular reason) would not show himself anymore. There were a few times when I might have seen him, but there were too many camera flashes from excited attendees to be positive of what I was seeing.

BLPA wrapped up the night by gathering the remaining guests into the main hall (with the fireplace) to conduct an EVP session. Two extremely sensitive microphones were connected to a laptop; one microphone went down into the basement and the other stayed in the main hall with us. Rick made everyone aware that complete and total silence was required, due to the high sensitivity of the microphones.

The session was short, consisting of only about twenty questions. He immediately replayed the recording and got a hit on the first question — "What is your name?" The reply was low, but clear. A female voice answered "Nancy." It was one of the few times that an entire group of people agreed on what was said…the first time it was played. With a small amount of filtering, the word remained unchanged. With an amazing ending, Rick announced the end of the event (which actually went two hours over!).

Rick Bugera (sitting in front of the laptop) performs a live EVP recording session. As the recording was taking place, everyone present could hear if a response was captured.

CONCLUSION

Although this site definitely warrants continued study, it seems that there are at least two spirits roaming the halls of the old hotel. Berks Lehigh Paranormal Association plans on holding several more "open to the public" ghost hunts at this location. If you have the chance, I do recommend that you attend. When you do decide to visit, be sure to bring along your camera and an audio recorder...and say "Hi" to Fred and Nancy for me!

Where It Is
Lake House Hotel is located at Route 115 and Cherry Valley Road, Saylorsburg, PA 18353

WEATHERLY

THE "HAUNTED" CEMETERY

Located just outside of Weatherly, Pennsylvania, on North Church Road is a small, forgotten cemetery. It is about a half-mile off South Lehigh Gorge Drive, tucked away in a heavily wooded area. Only pieces of an old iron fence surround it; no sign with a name stands at the entrance. In fact, there is nothing here to tell a visitor what cemetery this once was. Trees make up three sides of the cemetery while Church Road creates the front border.

I started visiting this "lost cemetery" after my in-laws told me about it. They had a friend stop by one day, and the conversation turned to what my wife and I do for a hobby. The friend had asked if we had ever visited the "haunted cemetery," a place that has been visited by locals (teens) for years.

The story goes something like this: back in the 1800s, an epidemic hit the area and many small children and infants passed away. A mass grave was dug in the center of this cemetery and the bodies were placed within. After some time, when people would visit the cemetery at night, they supposedly could hear the voices of the children's mothers singing a lullaby. "Hush little baby, don't say a word..."

In July 2000, I was staying at the in-laws for a weekend. My father-in-law had mentioned the place to me, and also that he knew where it was. So, we jumped in the car and followed the directions (given by

The Haunted Cemetery — After a light snowfall, the details of where the graves are can easily be seen by the many ups and downs in the ground.

the friend) to the cemetery. After getting lost, we eventually found it. I walked around the outside of the cemetery, checking for "No Trespassing" or "Private Property" signs. Finding nothing to stop us from going onto the grounds, we proceeded to wander among the headstones.

Let me tell you, this place looks like it *should* be haunted! The grass was overgrown and many of the older headstones, which dated back to the 1820s, have been knocked over and/or broken off their bases. Some were even buried under grass and brush. To say the least, the place was in really bad shape. Personally, this kind of stuff really bothers me — that the places we hold "sacred" for our deceased loved ones are so easily forgotten and basically disregarded.

I decided to come back that night for my own, private ghost hunt. Around 9 o'clock, my wife, mother-in-law, and grandmother (in-law) piled into the car and headed back. They had expressed interest in going on a "ghost thingy" and since this wasn't a formal investigation...hey, why not! Besides, my mother-in-law has the strangest luck; you never know what might happen when she's around.

I parked my car and we began making our way through the scattered and broken headstones. I snapped off a few pictures here and there; the others did the same. A few times I felt a cold chill sort of go by me, like someone walking by. However, this cemetery was out in the middle

This is an example of what's left of the fence that used to surround the cemetery. Rusted and broken sections dot the borders of this somewhat forgotten place of rest.

of nowhere *and* on top of a mountain, so it could have been just my imagination. I moved on, and every few minutes, I would stop and look into the woods surrounding the cemetery. I had the strong feeling that I was going to see people emerge from the darkness of the trees. I had heard movement in the woods, but I was attributing them to animals. However, the feeling that someone was going to walk out kept getting stronger. At one point, I planted my feet and waited a good ten minutes, staring at one section. Nothing emerged, and the feeling soon faded away.

Towards the end of the night we stopped to do a Q&A recording session. My wife was taking photographs as I asked several questions. I even began singing a little bit of the lullaby that the story claims is heard here. As I was singing the lullaby, my wife's camera stopped working. She had just taken the last picture in the roll when it started acting weird. She got the roll rewound and when it was done, so was the camera. It refused to operate at all. After inserting a new roll of film, we tried different batteries to get it to work — eight freshly charged batteries, two at a time — with the same results. I even took out the batteries from my own camera, which was still operating normally, and placed them in her camera — nothing.

It has become an almost common sign of the presence of an entity; when electrical devices will begin to malfunction, or even suffer a complete loss of power. This is an event that I've experienced on many past investigations. In a normal, rational experience, a device that loses power can usually be fixed with a fresh set of batteries (or plugged into an outlet). However, it seems that a spirit has the ability to disrupt the normal flow of electricity (since some devices act weird, rather than simply shutting off). It would seem that on this night, we were not alone.

It was at this time that I began to get that feeling again…only this time there were many people around us, all standing just inside the darkness of the trees.

With my wife's camera malfunctioning — and the constant feeling of people around us — we decided to wrap things up. I got my gear and we all went back to the in-laws' house. My wife was telling everyone (there were a few guests at the house) about the camera suddenly not working. When she went to show them, it was working fine! It had the same batteries that were in it when it died at the cemetery, but now it seemed to be in perfect operating condition. Perhaps the children that are said to be buried there had decided to play a joke on us. Or maybe they were just interested in the camera, of which I'm sure they've never seen the likes of before.

Over the next several months, I had been visiting the "Haunted Cemetery" every couple of weeks. One time around, as I was traveling down North Church Road, I noticed a woman outside of her house, doing some lawn work. This house was the only one on the road, so I decided to stop and ask about the cemetery. The woman, who we will call "Jill," was able to tell me

An example of the terrible vandalism that has taken place here.

The last remnants of the church that used to be on this spot.

that it used to be St. Nicolas' Catholic Cemetery. There was a church on the grounds of the cemetery where only a flagpole now stands (without a flag). The church burned down around 1967 or 1968. According to the locals I spoke with, the fire was started by teenagers that had broken into the church in order to steal antique statues that decorated the interior.

Jill had also heard the story of a lot of children passing away around the 1800s due to a diphtheria plague near the turn-of-the-century. As I later found, a large number of the headstones are dated to the early 1800s. This lends a little validity, at least to the historical part, to the story of the Haunted Cemetery.

I thanked Jill and continued on to the cemetery, where I spent the majority of the day cleaning it up. Since I was coming here quite often, I wanted to help out a bit. I picked up some trash and unearthed some headstones that probably hadn't seen the light of day for years. I had just cleaned off a headstone with the family name of "Quinn" and turned around to pick up the trash bag I was filling...when I heard a voice behind me (from where the headstone was located).

"Thank you, Sir."

I froze. You know the feeling... when something startles you so much that your body goes rigid. That's what happened to me. It was so unexpected; in the late afternoon...in broad daylight...and not another soul around that I could see, suddenly a voice comes out of the air, *thanking me* for cleaning up. After the initial shock, I felt a sense of satisfaction that this spirit found a way, from the flip side of life, to say "Thank You" to me. I did the only thing I could think of...

I said, "You're Welcome." After waiting a few minutes to see if the conversation would continue (it didn't, much to my disappointment), I went back to cleaning up.

In April 2003, I arrived with Bob, a friend and former PIRA team member. After I had told him the stories and what I had experienced on past visits, he was itching to visit the place for himself. We arrived late on a Saturday night, and got to work setting up motion sensors in several locations around the cemetery. We set up a total of six sensors, all of the passive infrared type, starting at about twenty feet from where we parked the car. There is a small space on the far side of the lot where you could just about fit two cars. The sensors were spaced out approximately every ten feet along our path, all facing the same direction. Once the sensors were in place, we began to methodically make our way around the cemetery, stopping at specific locations to take readings, photographs, and recordings.

There were two separate occasions where our motion sensors activated, sounding an alarm. Each of these times, three to four alarms went off, which was very exciting because they were set up to cover a long area — as in a

The area the author was in when he experienced an audible EVP.

path that if you were to walk down, you would set an alarm off every ten feet you walked. The alarms were directed towards the cemetery, and not the road (even though there wasn't a single vehicle that came by). We re-created the event by walking along the path ourselves and setting the alarms off. Though not a "scientific" test, we judged the timing in which we were setting off the alarms to closely match what had happened earlier.

This caused us to set up our other equipment in this area, including audio recorders, video cameras, EMF (Electromagnetic Field) meters, and temperature meters. However, once we sat down and started our EVP (Electronic Voice Phenomena) recording session, the activity simply ceased. It literally felt like a switch had been thrown and anything paranormal had just been turned off. Luckily, I had my digital recorder on the entire time there was activity going on. When I reviewed the recordings later that night, I found that I had captured two EVPs. The first one is a male voice that, to this author, sounds as if it's saying, "Do you like wine?" We weren't asking questions at the time; we were simply walking to another site and talking. I'm not sure if the spirit was asking us if we liked wine, or perhaps another ghostly friend walking the cemetery.

The second EVP sounds like it is from a female, though we have no idea what she is saying. I've tried several approaches (slowing down, filtering, increasing specific frequencies, etc.), but have yet to determine what is being said. I've come to the conclusion that she is speaking a language other than English, possibly German.

Since my last visit, "POSTED" signs have been put up everywhere. This photo was taken from the road. (My policy is to never trespass.)

Over the next year, I had many chances to go back and perform further investigations. The activity was sporadic, with nothing occurring for several consecutive visits. Then there would be a night when phantom footsteps would be followed by the sound of children giggling. Needless to say, the cemetery proved to be a very interesting place and had become one of my favorite sites to visit.

However, my relationship with the cemetery was not meant to last. In July 2004, an article in a local newspaper made some accusations towards ghost hunters. The article was about the anniversary of the cemetery, its history, and its current condition. What is sad is that the article grouped ghost hunters in with local teens who would use the cemetery for their late-night drinking parties — 40-ounce beer bottles were a common sight in the cemetery. What was insulting is that the article actually included a link back to my own website! I suspect this was because I had posted updates on my adventures to the cemetery. Since I'm not the type of person to keep quiet, I made my way back to the town of Weatherly to speak to those quoted in the article. I was able to voice my opinion and assure them that I was NOT responsible for the current condition of the cemetery.

When I spoke to the Pastor of the church that owns the cemetery, he made it quite clear that he did not want anyone on the grounds at night. In addition, he asked that only people attend during the day if they had religious or genealogical reasons. Absolutely no parties — and *no* ghost hunting. With that statement, my investigations at the "Haunted Cemetery" came to an end. It is the policy of my team, as well as myself, that we do not trespass — no exceptions.

CONCLUSION

While gathering stories for this book, I found myself in the Weatherly area once again. It had been almost four years since the last time I saw the place, and I was wondering if they had done anything to improve the site (and I wanted to grab some better photographs for the book). When I arrived, I was doubly disappointed; not only was the cemetery still in bad shape, but there were now signs on every tree stating, "POSTED — Private Property." Unfortunately, it seems that the cemetery remains off limits... for now.

As a matter of respect, I must ask that you do not go against the wishes of the cemetery owners. Since the land is POSTED, you could very easily be arrested and charged with trespassing should you decide to do a little ghost hunting on your own. Be aware that this is now strictly forbidden, and if caught, they will prosecute. However, one can still view the entire cemetery *from the road...*

6

KEMPTON

NEW BETHEL CHURCH CEMETERY

y first visit to New Bethel Church Cemetery took place in 1998. I had just read the book *Ghosts of Berks County* by Charles Adams, III (1982). Although I had read many books on ghosts prior to this one, this was the first book I had actually purchased on the subject and it was the first one to make an impression on me. The story of Hawk Mountain and Matthias Shambacher had finally inspired me to get out and start *looking* for ghosts...rather than just reading about them.

So, with my trusty, worn, and weathered book in hand, I took a road trip with my wife and family. On the way up, I filled the family in on the reason the cemetery is said to be haunted. In the 1800s, a man named Matthias Shambacher owned a tavern on what is now called Hawk Mountain, located in Berks County, Pennsylvania. The tavern was a welcome rest stop for those traveling over the mountain, with the offer of Blue Mountain Tea and applejack to refresh the body. However, Mr. Shambacher had a nasty reputation among the locals. Time and again, he was accused of murdering many of the travelers after leaving the tavern. In the end, as he lay dying, he confessed to killing an unknown amount of men. The bodies of these men were never recovered, so no one ever knew exactly how many lives Matthias may have taken during his killing spree.

New Bethel Church Cemetery...as viewed from the top of the hill.

Along with the rumors of these murders, there is a strange tale associated with the burial of Matthias. On the day he was laid to rest, a sudden and fierce storm rolled over the mountain towards the grave. Just moments before, the skies had been clear and blue. Lightening is said to have struck the grave, not once but several times. Those in attendance took this as an obvious sign, believing that God himself was showing his disapproval.

Since that time, there have been sightings of the paranormal-type for many years. Glowing lights have been witnessed hovering over headstones and then either fading away or zipping off into the woods. Another account has the figure of a man standing, staring down at the grave (of Matthias), only to walk up the hill and disappear. Stories of strange voices and a screaming woman have also circulated about this cemetery.

Not too long ago, I had the chance to hear Mr. Adams speak at a convention. At my request, he told the story of Matthias, adding on an experience of his own. As he told it, he had organized a bus tour with New Bethel Cemetery being one of the stops. The bus pulled over, and everyone gathered out onto the roadside. As Mr. Adams was telling a story to the group, he noticed that people were getting very excited and/or scared, with some getting up and returning to the "safety" of the bus. When Mr. Adams stopped

A view of the cemetery from the road, with the unmarked grave of Matthias Schambacker in the center of the first row. There is only a base, no headstone.

talking, the remaining guests started to point at the graves behind him. As Mr. Adams turned around, he saw a shaft of blue light hovering over the grave of Matthias Schambacker. It hovered for a few moments, and then faded until there was no trace of it. That was probably one of the best "ghost tours"...ever!

It seems that the cemetery has a lot of experiences to offer those who are brave enough to visit at night. What I would like to do here is recount my own experiences at the cemetery. Over the years, I've visited the cemetery more times than I can remember. Although most of the time I go out there on my own, I've had the pleasure of being joined by members of my team (PIRA), as well as several other paranormal teams around the area. Most of my adventures to New Bethel have been documented on my website, but changes in format and adding newer cases have put these stories on the "back burner." When I began gathering stories for this book, I thought it would be a perfect place to tell them once again. Although not in the Allentown or Bethlehem area, it's only a short drive southwest to Hawk Mountain. And I firmly believe you'll find the cemetery worth the drive. So, here it goes...

The first time I visited New Bethel, I must admit that I could not find the headstone of Matthias Shambacher. I was a little embarrassed since I had just drug my wife and in-laws on an forty-five-minute drive to see this place and now I wasn't even sure if it was the right place. We were on New Bethel Church Road, so I was pretty sure this was it, since it was the only church and graveyard on the road. Keep in mind that this was a time before GPS units were a common item to keep in your car.

During the course of a two-hour search of every headstone, we found that one — *and only one* — stone was missing from its base. At first, this trip was deemed uneventful. We decided to call it a day and grab a bite to eat. Although I was supposed to be the "ghost hunter," we were all surprised when my mother-in-law developed her film and caught two photographs showing anomalies. It appeared to be a mist (Ectoplasmic Mist?) that changed positions and shape between the two photographs. Whether it was coincidence or an intentional sign, the mist appeared over the grave with the missing headstone. These "mists" were more solid, looking more like puffy clouds than a mist. Although one might try to explain these things as low lying clouds, their position would have put them in between us and the lower section of the cemetery. Not only would they have been obvious to us, but they also would have been "in the way" as we headed back to the car.

Feeling that there was definitely something going on at New Bethel — and being a little jealous that my mother-in-law got a couple of cool photographs — I planned another weekend road trip. This time around, I had my Polaroid camera, a micro-cassette recorder, 35mm camera with 200-speed color film, and my EMF meter. I was absolutely determined that this time I would capture something! Ah… so young I was.

I always make it a point, when possible, to swing by an investigation area during the day. This allows me to see what's going on, if there are any dangers I needed to be aware of, or even find some interesting new things to explore. Luck was with me this time around because on this day I met up with a man who actually helped run the church. I explained why I was there, which brought a look of worry to this man; apparently they have had many problems with vandals caused by the ghost stories. After some more conversation and explaining that I was only there to take pictures, he finally revealed the reason why I couldn't find the headstone of Matthias Shambacher — it had been broken off by vandals! I believe the stone was replaced once, but after being vandalized again, the staff decided to keep the headstone in storage. I was feeling much better now that I had confirmation that this really was the right place, so I left for the day, with the intention of going back that night.

I arrived back there about 8:45 p.m. I pulled out my EMF meter and began to take readings in a grid-like pattern around the grave of Matthias. At first, nothing registered above 1mg. I stopped for a moment, holding the meter in my hand while I decided where to go next. While standing still, the meter steadily went from a non-existent reading to a 9 (the scale reads from 0.1 to 10mg) and back down to 0...all within a matter of about ten seconds. A few minutes later, the same thing happened again. I was so excited!

This cemetery is out in the middle of nowhere and I could not find a natural source for the way the meter was acting. It was similar to when I would walk past, say, a personal computer with the meter on. As I approached, the meter would progressively read higher until it peaked (when I came closest to the computer) and started to diminish as I walked away. The only difference here was that I was standing still and the electromagnetic field was *approaching me* and then moving away. Was someone or something walking by me, perhaps checking out what I was doing?

On the third and final time this strange event took place, it got a little scarier. I had taken a few photographs while the meter was again on the rise, when all of a sudden an intense feeling came over me — a feeling of "I better get the hell out of here." I wasn't spooked or scared because I was in a graveyard alone...it was more like an urgent need to get away because something that was NOT NICE was coming. I was suddenly hit with the idea that for the last few minutes something was stalking me and now it was ready to strike. I do not hold a belief in psychic abilities, but I do know when to listen to my instincts. I grabbed my gear and got back to my car rather quickly. And then I waited, hoping to see the "NOT NICE" thing come out so maybe, just maybe, I could get a picture of it. Sadly, nothing came shrieking out of the woods...

When I got the pictures back (yes, in the old days of using film, we had to wait for the negatives to be developed), I found that I had two shots that turned up something. One showed a white orb — however, I no longer consider orbs to be evidence of the paranormal. The other photograph shows a red anomaly that seemed to be coming out of the ground of another grave. The area around the anomaly appears to be illuminated by it, giving it a very eerie look. Unfortunately (and thus the credibility of this statement will decline), the photographs I had were destroyed in a basement flood I had two years ago (which is why they have not been included here).

JULY 22, 2000

I went back to New Bethel Cemetery again. I was once again by myself since my wife experiences what she describes as "a bad feeling" whenever she visits this site. I arrived around 10 p.m. and I admit I was a little hesitant about walking out there. Along the front of the cemetery is the street and on the other side of the street is a small parking area, which was where I was now parked and standing. I had gathered my gear, threw the backpack over my shoulder, turned towards the cemetery, and…simply stood there. Once again, I had the feeling like something was there — *it was NOT NICE* — and that I was going to be in some serious trouble if I walked across the street. It was truly a strange sensation; I'm a big guy and there is little in this world to which I can truly say, "I'm afraid of." Ghosts are not one of them, and certainly an empty cemetery is not either.

However, here I was, feeling almost nauseated at the thought of having to walk a mere twenty feet with absolutely no visible signs of danger.

I kept thinking, "What the hell is going on here?"

After walking up and down the side of the road for what seemed like an hour (more like five minutes), the feeling I was having simply vanished, as if someone snapped their fingers and POOF…it was gone. I was now able to walk up the hill and say "Hello" to my favorite dead guy, Matthias. As usual, he remained shy and wouldn't respond. So, I started to snap some photos in the area.

I recall making a comment along the lines of, "Hey Matty, what the hell? You can kill a bunch of people, but you're scared as hell of me?" Almost instantly, I felt the ambient temperature drop. The thermometer I was carrying went from a nice 82 down to 64 degrees. A sound came from the top of the hill, like an animal crying out. It lasted for a few minutes, sounding over and over. It reminded me of a movie scene in which a woman wept over the loss of her husband. Strange, to say the least. I waited, snapping photos over the next five minutes. The temperature slowly returned to the previous reading of 82 degrees and the wailing suddenly ceased. All was quiet…all was warm again.

I was a little unnerved by this event. It made me feel as though I was in a movie myself! I thought, "Don't run from the hockey mask (he catches you anyway), don't fall asleep, and aim for the brain…it's the only thing that kills them." Yeah, funny things to think about at that time. I shrugged it off and continued my investigation.

I walked around most of the older part of the cemetery, finally ending up by the grave of Matthias again. I started taking pictures again when I was once again enveloped by an intense cold. Almost by instinct alone, I pressed the shutter on my camera. Just as the flash went off, I again got a strong feeling that it was time to leave.

It was getting late and I still had a forty-minute ride to where I was staying. The photo that I captured by that "instinctive" button push revealed a misty image that resembled a skeletal hand covering the majority of the image. It's a creepy image, but I cannot be sure of what it truly is.

This photo was captured during an investigation after getting a "feeling." To me, it has the look of a skeletal hand, but that could just be my imagination.

APRiL 21, 2001

Bob, Donna, and I spent a few hours at my favorite cemetery. One of the strange things we experienced were pockets of hot air. Some were warm, but a few I walked through were really hot. They were just small areas that seemed to be stationary, with a higher temperature. The cemetery is on an open field on the side of a hill. This may very well be a natural occurrence, but I mention it here because it's the first time I've experienced it.

At one point we walked up to the top of the hill, where the edge of the woods starts. As we approached, Donna stopped dead, grabbed my arm, and said there was something there. She hardly ever freaks like this, so Bob and I went in for a closer look. I had heard nothing, but Donna said she heard footsteps coming towards her and then saw a figure among the trees. She described it as all black with no features to speak of, but it did have the shape of a man (this experience took place well before the term "Shadow Person" became common).

The three of us walked down the line of bushes and trees until Bob stopped, signaling that he had heard something. We both took some photographs, then jumped into the trees. We saw nothing — no figures, no animals…nothing. Our photos were unable to capture any anomalies.

NOVEMBER 23, 2001

Once again, I was able to visit my "good friend" Matthias at New Bethel Cemetery. This time around, I was the guest of the Lehigh Valley Ghost Hunters Society. I joined Scott (the team leader) and his team as they recruited new members. Scott had decided to use the New Bethel cemetery as kind of a "proving ground" for people looking to join his group. Everyone who applied simply met at the cemetery; we received a short orientation and then took part in an informal investigation.

The author has experienced a lot of activity around this tall monument. It's usually while standing near it that the three-foot shadow entity is seen moving around the headstones further down the hill.

I was able to speak to a few new people, but most of all, I got to walk around New Bethel Cemetery. The group split up into smaller teams and I went with Hillary's (a team leader) group to the top of the hill, by a tall statue with an angel on the top. I've always had good results back here and this night was no different. I had the urge the whole time to keep looking up at the angel. I took two pictures and actually felt that this was enough (That's the odd part). The photos didn't reveal anything, but in the light of the flash, I caught sight of a face of a young girl. It appeared at the base of the angel statue, and seemed to be poking out from behind it (as if the child was hiding behind the statue). She had blonde hair, which looked messed up. I had the distinct impression this child was a run-away. A second after the initial surprise, I circled the monument looking for any clue as to the girl's identity...or at least another glimpse of her.

This is the first time I've encountered this young girl, and was extremely excited to find out more about her. In everything I've read about the cemetery, I've never seen anything mentioning a little girl. In all my visits since, I haven't seen her again. Hopefully, she'll show herself to someone again, someday.

If you go looking for this stone, it shouldn't be too hard to find. It's in the last row and is the tallest monument there. All I ask is that you be respectful, so that we may continue to visit the site.

APRIL 15, 2006

On this trip, Greg and Rachael, part-time members of PIRA, joined me on my latest visit. I had mentioned that I'd be in the area, and since they didn't live too far away, I invited them up. I showed Rachael and Greg where the infamous grave of Matthias Shambacher was located, then headed up to the top of the hill, to the very last row of headstones. We settled in the area where I had previously seen the image of a young girl (well, just her face). Since this was more-or-less a relaxed ghost hunt rather than an investigation, it was more informal then usual.

The three of us sat for a while, taking random photographs and video footage of the headstones surrounding us. There were no unusual noises or sightings to report. We moved around the top rows of headstones, simply taking random shots and discussing past activity and other general topics.

We gathered together for an EVP session. Greg was designated the Q&A guy this time around. He did pretty well for his first time, asking questions that covered a wide range of information. This session lasted about ten to fifteen minutes. However, about one minute in, my audio

It's been down this row of headstones that many people — including this author — have witnessed a three-foot tall shadowy figure move towards the woods...only to disappear before making it there.

recorder shut off. It still had over thirty minutes of space left on it, so there was no reason for it to stop. I hit the record button again and it continued to record the rest of the session. When I reviewed the recording later on, I had obtained a rather interesting EVP. A very angry voice yelled, "Get that thing out of here!" And that's where the recorder had shut off. Interesting, wouldn't you say?

We closed the recording session and moved about the cemetery separately for a few minutes. After checking the time, we decided to pack it up. On the way down the hill, I caught movement between rows of headstones. It was about three feet tall, but looked like it was hunched over and running away from us. This may very well have been some kind of animal; however, I did not see it actually leave the area. It was running towards the woods, but never made it. It pulled one of those vanishing tricks about ten feet from the edge of the woods.

As we approached the area, we started recording. Greg had a significant power drain on his video camera, from ¾ to ¼ battery power. Both Greg and I experienced a drop in temperature at this time as well. My video camera displayed the "Low Battery" symbol and then went dead. (Upon returning home that night, I found the battery still had forty-eight minutes left on its charge.) I searched the ground for prints, but found nothing.

Although no stories are associated with this statue, I have always found it interesting. Perhaps one day I'll find out why.

CONCLUSION

This cemetery definitely has my interest. So many events go on here that it would certainly warrant a full-time investigation. From wailing sounds to columns of light...it's a ghost hunter's dream. I look forward to visiting this site for years to come...as long as we don't get banned.

Please, always show respect for these places. It is where we lay our loved ones to rest. One day, you'll be doing the same, so keep that in mind when ghost hunting.

And...In speaking with an associate, Jeff (head of NAPA), later on, I found that he has also witnessed a three-foot tall thing move through the cemetery. Jeff described it going into the underbrush, but making no noise at all. I believe this is something to keep our eyes out for...

FREEMANSBURG

FREEMANSBURG CEMETERY

J ust east of Bethlehem lies the small town of Freemansburg. A friend of mine, Bob (a former member of PIRA), lives just a few blocks away from a tiny graveyard simply known as Freemansburg Cemetery. (Honestly, this is what we believe the cemetery is named. There are no signs indicating the actual name.) Bob had always wanted

The Freemansburg Cemetery...with it's one and only tree.

The tree of the Red-Haired boy.

to investigate this site, telling me many times that he would get an "eerie" feeling every time he drove past it. For years, we never got the chance to walk through the extremely small cemetery.

However, thanks to the book you're reading now, I started traveling to the area more often (I live in Philadelphia, Pennsylvania). It was during one of my adventures that I found myself a few minutes away with some time to spare. I pulled around and parked my minivan along side of the cemetery and got out. I was there for about ten minutes when I noticed a young man watching me from one edge of the grounds. I made my way over to him and introduced myself. After telling him about my search for ghost stories, and finally getting to visit this place after several years, my new friend, Kevin, asked if I was here about the little redheaded kid.

"Well...sure. What can you tell me?" was my response. Yeah, I had no idea what he was talking about, but hey, it sounded like a story!

Kevin claims to have had three experiences while walking up Monroe Street, always taking place just around sunset. His first run-in with the "Red-Headed Kid" took place about ten years ago while he was out for a nightly walk. He was on his way home from a friend's house, his route taking him past the cemetery. The sun had begun to sink and the sky had turned a red-orange color. The quiet of the night was broken by the sound of laughter. As he looked to his right, Kevin saw a small boy skipping around the tree. The boy was unfamiliar, but one thing really stood out about him — his bright red hair.

Kevin wasn't sure if it was because of the sunset or simply a trick of light, but he described the boy's hair as almost being on fire! Although it was getting harder to see with the setting sun, the flaming head of hair stood out as the boy kept skipping around the tree. Mesmerized by what he was seeing, Kevin had actually stopped walking and simply stood in the road, watching the boy.

As the kid went behind the tree once again, he failed to come out the other side. Kevin stood there for a minute, confused as to where the boy was. The tree stands alone in the center of the cemetery, so there was no place for the kid to hide. With his curiosity eating at him, he changed direction and headed straight for the large tree. Once there, he found that the boy with the fiery hair was gone. Looking all around, there was simply no trace of the kid. After staring around for a few more minutes, Kevin finally continued his journey home.

The second encounter came several years later. After a disagreement with his wife, Kevin needed to get some fresh air, so he went for a walk. Thinking about the argument and not paying attention to where he was going, he found himself at Freemansburg Cemetery. He remembered his experience with the redheaded kid and decided to go sit at the base of the tree for a while. Kevin admits that he was hoping the kid,

Looking down the hill of the cemetery.

which he now believes is a ghost, would make another appearance. However, after an hour or so, there was no sign of anyone coming out of the cemetery.

Kevin picked himself up and headed home. As he reached the edge of the cemetery, he heard laughter from behind him. Spinning around, he saw the little boy once again, skipping his way around the tree, his hair looking like a small inferno. This time around, Kevin wanted to get a closer look before the boy disappeared again. He began walking towards the center of the cemetery, and that is when things changed.

As the boy emerged from the left side of the tree, he stopped, grabbed onto the tree, looked directly into Kevin's eyes, and ... smiled. Kevin related to me that he felt a connection at that moment, like they were supposed to meet. The boy's smile faded, and he moved back behind the tree...and was gone. Once again, Kevin walked around the tree, looking for any clue to where the boy could have gone. Sadly, there was nothing.

Kevin's final experience took place about four months before we met. It had become a routine for him to come out to the cemetery every two or three days, in the hopes that he would see the redheaded kid again...and maybe get a little closer than the last time. I'll let Kevin's own words describe what happened.

> "It was a Thursday, just before sunset. I was walking around the outside edge of the cemetery, didn't want to go in 'cause he never came out while I was in there. I guess I walked around the place four times when I heard the kid laughing. When I looked over at the tree, there he was...just standing there and staring back at me. He was smiling and rocking back and forth on his heels. I started to walk to him, and his smile went away...replaced by a sad face. I gotta tell ya, I was worried...like I did something wrong. I started to walk to him again, and it looked like he was going to cry! I figured this meant I should stay put, so I turned around, and walked back to the edge of the cemetery. When I looked back, he was smiling again. He surprised me again by waving at me, before turning round and skipping around the tree. He only went behind it once; he didn't come out the other side. That was the last I saw of him...so far."

CONCLUSION

I walked around the cemetery for some time after speaking with Kevin. I found nothing that would give me a clue as to who this redheaded boy could be. Kevin tells me he has done a little research,

A close-up of the tree that supposedly is where a boy with fiery red hair will walk around the base.

but he also came up empty-handed. For the time being, Kevin has named the kid "Charlie" because, as he says, "He looks like a Charlie to me, so his name's Charlie...until he tells me otherwise."

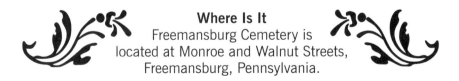

Where Is It
Freemansburg Cemetery is located at Monroe and Walnut Streets, Freemansburg, Pennsylvania.

EAST WEISSPORT

THE HOUSE OF THE HANGING MAN

My first encounter with the "House of the Hanging Man" came after I had been on an all-day adventure with my friend Greg and his team, Eastern Pennsylvania Paranormal Investigations. We had finally arrived back from a very (very) long day and I was about ready to head home when Greg mentioned this house, which happened to be right down the street from one of his members. When I was asked if I wanted to take a look, I was already grabbing my camera. Hey, even when I'm dead tired, I'll get a "second-wind" to check out another potentially haunted site.

Yes, I did say *haunted*. Although I, nor the others, were aware of it at the time, there were a few stories attached to the abandoned home. Days after visiting the site, I had posted some of the photos on my Explorers Club website, which is dedicated to documenting abandoned buildings otherwise forgotten or ignored in the present day. It wasn't long before I received a few emails telling me of some very interesting experiences.

The stories go something like this: In 1982 or 1983, the house was a rental property. A man, said to be in his forties, had moved into the house during the fall. He immediately drew attention from neighbors because he moved in all of his belongings only after

This is all that's left of the House of the Hanging Man. The front section of the house was torn down some time ago.

dark. The gossip mill had started, with rumors that this man must be a shady character. He never came out during the day, but he could be heard. Local kids that would venture too close would run away in a panic when a deep roar would come forth from the open windows. "Get Away or I'll Shoot Ya Dead!" is what they would hear. The voice was described as deep and scratchy, like someone who had smoked two packs a day for the better part of his life.

Soon, the kids got a little braver...daring each other to get closer and closer to the house. According to the story, it became a sort of "Right of Passage" to sneak up to the house and knock on the partly opened kitchen window. Although most never made it half way across the yard, a few got the scare of their lives. It is said that those who made it to the window, would reach out their hand to knock...then suddenly be grabbed by a large, dirty hand that would shoot out of the window with tremendous speed. The grip was like fire and, struggle as those kids would, they would be pulled even closer to the window. Then, to add to the absolute horror, a dirty and distorted face would appear in the window. "I

SAID STAY AWAY! STAY AWAY!" At this point, you can imagine that the child was ready to pee himself.

However, there was one kid who, when he broke free of the man's grip, stood his ground. According to the story, the teenager shouted back at the man, "Why don't you go away?! No one wants you here! Why don't you just kill yourself!" To the boy's amazement, the man in the window said nothing, and moved out of view. For the next few days, no one saw or heard from the scary man. Then about a week later, a nauseating odor made its way from the house... the smell of death was in the air. The police were called and they managed to get into the house. The interior was like a junkyard; trash piled up everywhere, food and beer cans all over, and junk filled every available open space. When they reached the Dining Room, they found the owner — hanging from a rope tied to the ceiling fan, a knocked-over chair directly under him. Rumors say he couldn't take the constant abuse and finally took his own life. But this is a book about ghosts, so our story is not over yet!

Years later, it had become known as the Hanging House and had a reputation for being haunted. The original owner never acquired

The kitchen area...where the face of an angry man can be seen looking out.

The chair that we found in the dining room area.

another renter, and so the house was left empty...except for the kids. Local teenagers now considered the place as their very own "hang-out," a place to drink and do all the things that teenagers do. This is where the stories of the Hanging Man started.

At first, groups of kids looking to party would occasionally see the dirty face of an angry man floating in the window. As you would expect, this had many boys and girls changing their minds about entering this house! However, some were brave enough to still head in. Once inside, the majority of the partygoers would be treated to another apparition. A large man, kind of hunched over, would be standing in the kitchen and staring out the window. He would then turn, look at the kids with a distorted face, and begin yelling...only no sound could be heard. The fear and terror the kids were feeling would now be mixed with confusion. The angry apparition looked as if he was screaming at the top of his lungs... yet nothing but silence came forth. Needless to say, the parties usually ended right about that time!

This view from another angle shows the chair...under the fan. Could this be where the poor man took his own life?

The last encounter from these stories is perhaps the most disturbing of all. Two young couples decided to spend a few quiet hours inside the house, where they could "be alone" for a while. They were gathered in the dining room area, laughing and having a great time, when one of them heard a creaking noise from above.

When they looked up, they were treated to a horrific sight: a large man, hanging by his neck from the ceiling fan, gently swaying back and forth.

The kids could do nothing but sit there in stunned silence, too scared to move or speak. The body slowly turned, creaking as it moved. It only lasted a few seconds and then the image faded away. The kids, finally regaining control of their motor functions, screamed as they ran out of the house.

Of course, these stories are unconfirmed at this time. The house, as it was during my visit in 2008, had been left abandoned for several years. There is still trash in the house, but there was plenty of room for myself, Greg, and several members of his team. We piled into the house and spread out, searching the house for clues as to who used to live there.

At the time of my visit, I had not yet learned of these stories. We were simply checking out an old and (very) obviously abandoned house on the edge of town. Walking past the kitchen and into the dining room, we came upon an odd sight: a single chair, positioned in the middle of the room, under the ceiling fan. At the time, we had joked about someone thinking of hanging themselves... (*remembering the chair, but forgetting the rope*).

CONCLUSION

Even though my visit to the Hanging House was uneventful, it turned out to be a decent lead for a story in this book. I appreciate all the emails I received about the house, especially from two sisters who apparently live down the street!

Since this is an abandoned building, there is good reason why I cannot list the exact location; it's been left to the elements for a number of years, which makes it unsafe. I've ventured into places like this many times and there's always an area of the floorboards that is just waiting to give way beneath an unsuspecting explorer.

EASTON

A LOVED ONE'S VISIT

" **C** indy" contacted my team through one of our former members (thanks Bob!). She had recently lost her husband in a motorcycle accident, and now believed there was paranormal activity in her home. Some of the experiences she was having were directly related to her husband while others were something she could not understand. She reached out to Bob, knowing he was associated with a paranormal investigation team, and asked if we would come out and see what we could find.

As with all of our investigations, we first conducted an interview with the client. This allows us time to gather information about the client, the history, and experiences that have been going on. It had been just over a year since her husband passed away. It was still a tender subject, but Cindy assured us that this was something she wanted to do. She was on a mission: to have someone help her prove (to herself) that she wasn't crazy. She was seeing things in her home that both scared her, as well as brought her bittersweet comfort.

She began her story. It started with the name-calling. Every few nights, at random, Cindy would hear her name called from another room. Soon, she would hear the same voice calling to her only a few feet away. The voice, she was convinced, belonged to her late husband. She said this with the utmost confidence, which made it hard to believe it could have been anyone else. This activity came to a peak one night while Cindy was watching television. As she sat on the couch, she suddenly noticed something next to her. As she turned her head, she stared into the eyes of her late husband! She described it as just his head, with the image fading out down the neck. He was transparent, with a smoky-like texture to his image. He was smiling at her...then his image slowly faded out to nothing.

But, there was also *another* presence within the house that has also made itself known to Cindy and her family. It was a quiet night, and Cindy's sister was babysitting. It was around eleven o'clock when Cindy came home; as her sister was gathering her personal things so she could get home, suddenly there was a flash of light on the stairway, which caused both of them to look up. As they watched, a large form slowly floated down the stairway. It was a dark grey mist, constantly swirling within itself, like a storm cloud ready to burst. As it moved down the steps, the smoky mass began to take on a human form. Cindy tells me that it was definitely a male, but taller and more "built" than her husband was. She grabbed her daughter and the three of them ran out of the house, spending the night at her parent's house.

In December 2002, three team members and I ventured out to this quiet twin-home in Easton, Pennsylvania. We set up various video cameras and audio recording devices, and then split into two teams. We had decided to try an experiment to see if we could prove that one of the entities was her husband. Each team was given a set of specific questions, seven to be exact. Each question was personal to Cindy's family and none of my team had any chance of knowing the answers. However, since we were looking for specific answers, Cindy had written the answers on a sheet of paper, then sealed them in a secured envelope — the kind that had printing on the inside, keeping you from seeing the writing on the contents.

During one of the sessions, my team — consisting of Cindy, Bob, and myself — set up in the basement. Cindy had mentioned during her interview that she hated the feeling she got while down there, though she could not give an exact reason why. This information made the basement a place of interest. The three of us sat there, in the dark, for a good twenty minutes. I was scanning the area with a night vision scope, when I spotted one of the oddest paranormal sightings I've had to date...an arm — *just an*

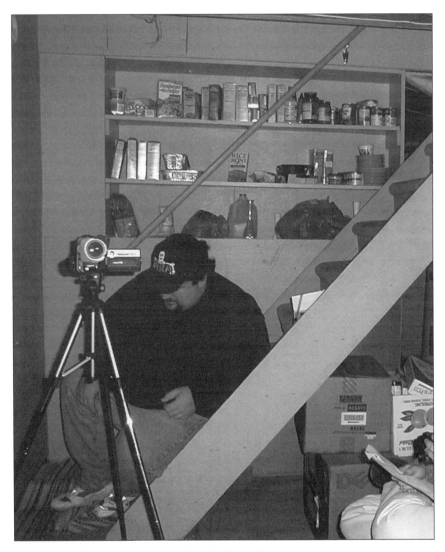

Investigating the basement area of a private residence.

arm — from midway between the shoulder and elbow down to the fingertips, was floating in the air. And...it seemed to be waving at me. It only lasted a few seconds, but was enough to get me excited and yelling at the other two about what I had just witnessed. The area it was coming from was behind an oil tank. A closer inspection yielded nothing out of the ordinary or a simple explanation for what I had seen. A strange experience, indeed!

The basement...where this author witnessed an arm waving at him.

After several hours, we decided to end the investigation with one more group session and everyone came together in the Living Room. It was just after ten o'clock, which was perfect — according to Cindy, the majority of activity happened between ten and eleven at night. We began our last session with some EVP questions. We asked our "Control" questions, then went on to asking some general questions. It was just about thirty minutes in, when Jim, another former member of PIRA, literally came flying down the main stairway. He had been sitting at the top of the stairway and honestly, I don't think he touched more than two of the steps in his rush to get down.

Once he calmed down a bit, he related what had happened. As we were asking questions, Jim had been looking into the two bedrooms he could see from his position. I asked if any spirits could show themselves, and if so, to make itself known. Well...*it* did. Jim said he got "that" feeling, the one you feel when someone walks up to you. He looked up and saw a dark figure take a step towards him, which put this entity right on top of him. It scared the crap out of him, to say the least! Jim has no doubt it was a male figure, but he said it looked like a "solid mist," swirling inside itself. (Take note, Jim was not present during my interview with the client, and it is our policy NOT to share the information with team members until after the first investigation. This is to eliminate any "influencing" of the investigators.)

After this experience, Jim refused to go back upstairs, so we decided to pack up and head home.

Investigator Jim...just before he witnesses a large figure loom over him.

CONCLUSION

When I had a chance to review the audio recordings, I found that we did obtain one EVP...and a strange one at that. It said the words "pig vomit," with some scratchy mumbling before and after. This EVP was recorded during the time we were asking the Control questions. We brought this information to Cindy, in order to get her input on what it could mean. I must say that I believed that the EVP was gibberish and didn't have any significance to the case. However, after hearing what we had recorded, Cindy called for us to bring out the sealed envelope that contained the answers to the Control Questions. I opened it up and scanned the paper inside... then smiled. The question we had asked was, "What is the name you gave to Bad Breath?"

The answer — "putrid *Pig Vomit* breath."

Cindy was in tears. For her, that was enough proof. Her tears were not of sadness, but of joy. Now she knew that he was ok, and apparently still looking over her from where ever he was. However, this left us with the question of *who or what* was the dark, misty figure that has been seen in the house? The descriptions didn't match her husband at all. So, who could it be?

Unfortunately, we'll never know. Cindy has since sold the house and moved on with her life. The house is still a private residence and I have not had any contact from the new owners. Perhaps they will see this and come forward with new stories of their own.

COPLAY

THE GHOST OF THE KILNS

G host stories can come from just about anywhere — and anyone. My search for tales of the other side has taken me all over the eastern side of Pennsylvania, in directions I really didn't expect, such as with someone I used to work with several years ago.

Jimmy is a levelheaded kind of guy who doesn't take much to "all those fairytales" about ghosts. In fact, whenever the subject of what I do for a hobby came up, he was always the first one to start harassing me…each and every time. So, it was a huge surprise to me when, after hearing that I was collecting ghost stories around the Allentown area, he called me up and said he had something to tell me—a ghost story he experienced himself. He began by telling me it took place while visiting the Coplay Cement Kilns.

Let's take a look at a little history…

In 1866, David O. Saylor (1827-1884) founded Coplay Cement Company near Allentown, Pennsylvania, where he constructed his first cement plant and pioneered the development of Portland Cement in this country. (Portland cement is the most commonly used cement around the world.) By 1871, Saylor was awarded his first American patent for high quality cement. Thinking ahead, Saylor purchased enough land not only for this first plant, but also for additional plants

The Coplay Cement Kilns.

for his company. As the demand for high quality cement grew, so did the Coplay Cement Company.

Unfortunately, Mr. Saylor would not be around to see it all; he passed away in 1884. However, the company did keep moving forward. In 1892, eight years after Saylor's passing, the management team at Coplay decided to construct a new mill in an effort to satisfy the growing demand for their product. A year later, the new mill, with eleven Schoefer kilns, roared to life. By the year 1900, over seventy-five percent of our nation's cement supply originated from this area.

The design of these new kilns was an advancement of earlier models, which were referred to as "bottle" or "domed" kilns. However, the technological wonder was short-lived...for just a few years later, the Atlas Cement Company developed and constructed the first Rotary Kiln in the United States. As business goes, this new invention saved the company money and labor costs. In 1904, the Coplay Cement kilns closed down, never to reopen.

Image of David Saylor, founder of the Coplay Cement Company in 1866. *Photo courtesy of Lehigh University.*

Of the eleven kilns originally constructed, only nine remain. The kilns were also housed in a large building, with only the tops of the kilns protruding through the roof. Everything but the nine kilns had been completely demolished. In its heyday, the area was filled with smoke, dust, noise, and more smoke. Today, all that remains of the factory are the tall, brick towers, which have long been silent and cold.

This was much like the day Jimmy visited the site with his kids. This was a day trip for the family because Jimmy and his kids are history buffs. They love delving into the history of the country, this area in particular. So, when they heard of the Kilns and realized that they weren't that far away, they hopped into the family minivan and off they went.

The day was overcast and a bit on the chilly side. The ruins of the kilns are located in a park, with walking paths and a playground. After some time at the playground on top of the hill, they made their way down to the kilns. While the kids ran and played among the base of the

A view from the back of the kilns.

kilns, Jimmy walked along the path. There are a few historical markers that share details of the Coplay Kilns' history. Jimmy was engrossed in what he was reading, when he became aware of his children talking to someone.

"You're clothes look really fancy, do you work here?"

"Yes, my dear…but it was a long time ago."

This exchange caught Jimmy's attention, as he had just read over the writing on the historical plaque: *In 1904, the fires of these Coplay kilns went out forever.* He looked up, thinking out loud, "How could anyone who worked at the kiln still be alive today?" Jimmy looked over at the kilns and saw his children and the man they were talking to, and a second thought hit him — "His clothes do look fancy…and old."

The man was wearing a suit, which was distinctly old-style. He wore a long, grey-white beard and sported a balding head. The man looked to be in his 50s, and walked slow and steady, looking up at each of the kilns one by one. The kids were off again, running between the kilns, but Jimmy kept his eyes on the old man, until he walked behind the kilns and out of sight.

A feeling of urgency swept over Jimmy, and all he wanted to do was to talk to this old man. He wanted to ask him his name, but had a strange feeling that the answer might freak him out. Nevertheless, he quickly walked, and then jogged, around to the opposite side of the kilns, expecting to easily "cut the old man off at the pass"…or path, as the park would have it.

The old gentleman was nowhere to be found. Jimmy ran (literally) around the kilns, then up the hill to the playground area, but could not locate the old man. Shaking his head in disbelief, Jimmy circled the kilns again, this time heading down the driveway towards the main street…still, the old man was simply gone.

This weird event left a deep impression on Jimmy, who, as we learned in the beginning of the story, is not one to believe in "fairytales" of ghosts. However, it wasn't until a few days later that his "fairytale" would make him a believer; he was going through the photographs on his camera and recalled the old man. He hadn't taken any pictures while the old man was walking around (Jimmy kicks himself for not thinking of doing that at the time), but he could at least look up any "ghost" stories associated with the kilns.

There were no tales of the paranormal to be found, but what he did find gave him the chills. On the monitor screen in front of him was an image of the man he saw. To Jimmy, it was unmistakable, but he called his kids over to have a look for themselves (and to verify what

Area where my friend Jimmy and his kids met the ghost of David Saylor.

A close-up of the kilns.

Jimmy already knew). Before he could get the question out, his youngest shouted, "That's the man in the fancy clothes!"

CONCLUSION

It seems that Jimmy and his kids had the rather unique opportunity to meet Mr. David O. Saylor, the former President of Coplay Cement Company...and who had passed away 124 years ago! Why the old man was wondering around the kilns, I have no idea. Perhaps it was simply to see how his kilns were doing...or perhaps to take simple pleasure in that fact that people were still interested in his kilns. Whatever the reason, if you visit the kilns yourself, you might have a chance to meet Mr. Saylor...in person.

Where is It
The Coplay Cement Company Kilns are on North Second Street in Coplay. The area is now Saylor Park, owned and run by Lehigh County. It's open Saturdays and Sundays from 1 to 4 p.m. and also by appointment. For more information, call 610-435-4664 or visit the website www.lehighcounty.org/Recreation/ and look for Saylor Park.

SCRANTON

THE HOUSE OF
THE STANDING KNIVES

In April 2005, I was invited to take part in an investigation hosted by Jerry of the Panther Valley Paranormal Society. His team had been to the site once before and wanted to follow up on the findings they had documented. I was called in to help with finding natural causes, as my area of "expertise" is debunking evidence. I'm not a total skeptic, but I keep a healthy dose of critical thinking and common sense in my backpack!

The site of this investigation took place in an old house built around the year 1902. There are four known previous owners to the house, with the original owners carrying the name of Miller. It is a large, three-story building with fourteen-foot ceilings and a total of thirty-two rooms, including bathrooms. We know that an older gentleman, somewhere in his 80s, passed away on the third floor of natural causes. All the floors have had some type of remodeling done, from removing of walls to partitioning rooms.

Before the investigation, Jerry filled me in on the reported activity, of which there's certainly been a lot! Odors of perfume and cooking — specifically onions and potatoes — have been detected throughout the entire house. The doorknob on the basement door has been observed turning back and forth with excessive force, as if someone was desperately trying to open the door. The basement door has been heard slamming shut...when it was already closed.

Between 4 and 5 a.m., a male voice has been heard stating, "Your case has already been decided." On several occasions, kitchen knives are left flat on a towel to dry after being washed. When the owners come back into the room, they find the knives standing up on their spines. Let me clarify: the knives are not stuck into the counter by the point — they are found standing up on their spines.

In the living room, a pale, white light is seen floating across the ceiling...only to disappear before the owners can find a source. A red light has also been witnessed in the same room, floating between the owners as they sit and watch television. Guests have reported feeling random cold and hot spots throughout the house. The TV in the main living room and an old door buzzer have been operating on their own since the new owners took over the house.

There has been a little girl seen sitting at the edge of the owner's bed. She is described as wearing a tiny, poofy-shouldered dress and sporting a ponytail. She never speaks nor makes any attempt to let anyone know why she's in the house. She would sit and just stare at the owners...until fading away.

Another figure has been seen. This one is a dark form. In one instance, one owner saw, reflected in a mirror, someone following him into the basement. When he turned to see who it was, no one was visible. The owners have also heard what sounded like children playing in the basement. Along with that, the owners heard (or got the impression) of music playing, glasses clinking together, and laughter of women.

Once we went over all of this information, we set up our equipment and split into two teams. After performing an experiment in the basement, a knife was found standing up on its spine. Unfortunately, no one had been paying attention to this area yet, so we set up two video cameras, both with night shot, to cover two different angles of a "set-up" area. Five knives were set up to test them. When we returned part way through the investigation, we discovered an interesting scene. Both video cameras had been turned off and were now pointed in different directions. The knives we had set up were now standing up on their spines. There were four investigators there, along with the two owners, that night. Everyone was accounted for during the course of the investigation and there were no other guests within the house at the time.

We reset the video cameras, along with the knives, and moved on to some EVP recording in some of the many rooms within the house. We first set up in the main bedroom. Instead of splitting up into teams, we decided to keep everyone together for these recording sessions (so we could keep an eye on everyone). Jerry began asking some questions, followed by the owners, and continued by me. There was an eight-degree drop in the temperature when I asked about the little girl appearing at the bottom of the bed.

CONCLUSION

Upon reviewing the recordings later on, I found an answer to one of my questions. I had asked, "What does your Mommy call you?" ... A reply of "Jessie" can be heard coming from the voice of a little girl.

Jessie has not been identified in research that the owners have been doing. In any case, the current owners have accepted her as a permanent houseguest. They also believe she is the entity responsible for the knives being moved around, as well as the rest of the activity in the house.

A LESSON
IN GHOST HUNTING SAFETY

I saved this short story for the end of the book, since the last story is usually the one you remember the most (besides your favorite one). I'll tell you up front that this is not a ghost story, per say — it is more of a "Heads-Up" for my fellow ghost hunters. You see, of all the attributes we associate with the hobby of ghost hunting and paranormal investigation, many teams forget something important — SAFETY.

Think about it... How many private residences has your team investigated where you really have no clue who the people are (except for what you got from a few emails)? Background checks, though it may sound funny, should be a part of your Preliminary Investigation. Depending on how your group, or you as an individual investigator, operates, you may find yourself in a less-than-desirable location, with people who turn out to be something from a "B-Movie" horror film. Although the following story doesn't go that bad, it will (hopefully) cause you to take a little extra precaution when setting up interviews and investigations.

It all started with an email. Most of them do, since the ghost hunting world is, in a very large part, Internet based. This email was a little different; the gentleman did not want an investigation, just simple documentation of a phenomenon he was experiencing in his apartment. He lived in the Poconos area and requested a meeting at my earliest convenience. Everything about the email — wording, presentation, style — suggested an intelligent man of sound mind. (Compared to other emails I get...you guys know the ones.) In the email, "Ed" stated that while watching TV, he would notice faces forming in the carpet — ranging from a woman wearing a veil to a figure he described as an alien being. (Due to privacy and legal concerns, "Ed" is the name we will be using to address him.)

Since I was already scheduled to be in the area to assist the Panther Valley Paranormal Society with another case, I contacted Jerry (head of the PVPS) and asked if he and his group would like to help me out (I never go to any investigation site alone). Jerry was up for it, and we met at his place for the trek up to the Poconos. Our first glimpse of the apartment was our first sign that this may be an issue. The place was unkempt, with trash and junk piled up against the walls. The place was not the most inviting location we had ever visited.

As we approached the front door, a plump man came out and greeted us with a great deal of enthusiasm...too much, we thought. As he led us inside, we found ourselves in a two-and-a-half room apartment. The place was very small, with the Living Room doubling as a Bedroom. Once inside the Living Room, I began asking Ed about the "faces" he's been seeing in the carpet. He immediately dropped down on his hands and knees, and began crawling around pointing at sections of carpet and telling us about the faces. Unfortunately, neither I, nor any of the PVPS members, saw these "faces." When I related this to Ed, his entire demeanor began to change...

Ed decided to relate to us that he was recently released from prison, but he "was much better now" (seriously, he actually said those words). His facial expressions began to change quickly, almost getting twitchy. He also related to us the crime that he was put away for...let's just say that you wouldn't want to invite this guy into your home. At this point, I asked the young ladies in our group to wait outside, leaving me, Jerry, and another male team member in there with Ed. There was one more thing that Ed wanted to show me, and we walked into the kitchen (Jerry and the other PVPS member waited in the Living Room). As I entered the kitchen, Ed moved around so that he was now between me and the doorway, which caused me to be a little concerned. He pointed to the wall, where there was an image scratched into the paint: a dagger with a snake wrapping around it. Ed went into a story of how he would scratch this image into his cell wall over and over again...and wanted to know if this was significant concerning spirit possession.

I said I'd like to discuss this with my associates and moved towards the doorway. At the same time, Ed moved to block my way. The manner in which he did this was clear — he was keeping me from leaving. This was "strike three" for Ed, and I asked him politely but firmly to get out of my way. I pushed past him, told the other guys it was time to go, and we simply left.

CONCLUSION

This was a situation that could — *and did* — happen. It started out as any other case, but turned into something that could have been a dangerous situation for me...if I had gone alone. Sure, the situation didn't escalate to violence, but I had the feeling it could have if I hadn't had the PVPS members as backup. In retrospect, I made a bad decision in following Ed into his kitchen. My curiosity of what he would say or show me next overrode my common sense — that it was a bad idea to be alone with this guy.

Hopefully, my experience will cause you to think twice before ever going out on a case alone. You never know what you're getting yourself into, so always stay cautious! I've made it a practice to do a search on a client's name and address, do a drive-by (if local), and leaving complete details of the location with family (so someone knows where you are). Also, above all else, always take someone else with you. It doesn't matter if they're a member of your team or not, take someone with you. I've taken my neighbor on an interview, as well as a co-worker once.

Bottom Line — Never go alone.

GHOSTLY SHORTS

This chapter contains what I've simply named Ghostly Shorts — very short stories about some of the more popular, well-known haunts in the Allentown and Bethlehem area. These little tidbits of spooky tales are offered for your enjoyment, but have not been verified yet. Perhaps I'll have the opportunity to visit some of these locations in the future.

KING GEORGE INN

The sound of a crying baby has been heard by guests coming from the kitchen area, as well as from an old well located in the basement. Also, the ghost of a woman in eighteenth century attire, carrying her baby, has been seen walking near the basement and around the kitchen. King George Inn is located at 3141 Hamilton Boulevard, Allentown, Pennsylvania 18103; visit its website at www.kinggeorgeinn.com.

CEDAR CREST COLLEGE

The story goes that in 1956 a woman named Wanda committed suicide inside the building known as Butz Hall. For years, witnesses have seen this young woman roaming the halls. Cedar Crest College is located at 100 College Drive, Allentown, Pennsylvania 19104.

INN AT MAPLE GROVE

Local legend says that a Native American was having an affair with a white woman who eventually became pregnant. He was lynched for what the townsfolk found to be an unspeakable crime. The body of the Native American is supposedly buried under the fireplace, but other reports have his body buried under the basement dirt floor. However, activity seems to increase with the lighting of that fireplace: whistling is heard with no apparent source, knocking sounds are heard, footsteps move about the dining room, and a heavy chandelier swings of its own accord. Much more activity has been reported over the years. The Inn at Maple Grove is located at 2165 State Street, Alburtis, Pennsylvania 18011.

MUHLENBERG COLLEGE

The ghost of the Bernheim House is believed to be that of the former owner, Oscar Bernheim. Oscar had a love of roses and kept a beautiful garden—full of roses—on the grounds. Oscar willed the house to the college with the condition that garden would continue to be tended to. After several years, it seems that this "condition" was forgotten. Two dormitories replaced the garden, as well as the house. The ghost of Oscar has been seen in the rooms of the South Hall dormitory. Other activity includes phantom noises that come from nowhere, TVs turning off and on by themselves, and objects being tossed about. Muhlenberg College is located at 2400 Chew Street, Allentown, Pennsylvania 18104.

HOTEL BETHLEHEM

Guests of the hotel report seeing strange shadows and apparitions moving about the rooms. Staff members have heard their names called out...only to find no one around when they search for the caller. Many guests have reported feeling someone tap them on the shoulder...only to find empty space when they turn around. The apparition of a small girl has been seen looking out one of the windows; she's believed to be the ghost of May Yohe, a well-known singer and actress during the 1890s who grew up living at the hotel. Although she died at the age of 69, many believe she cherished her childhood so much that she seems to have returned to her former home. The strangest event that occurs is the phantom vacuuming. It seems that the vacuums will turn on by themselves and start moving around the floor. Sometimes the vacuums aren't even plugged in! Hotel Bethlehem is located at 437 Main Street, Bethlehem, Pennsylvania 18018.

EASTON PUBLIC LIBRARY

During the construction of the library in 1903, over five hundred graves were uncovered at the site. Although most were relocated to other cemeteries, approximately thirty bodies that could not be identified were not. To put it simply, they were dumped together in an underground concrete vault, located somewhere on the property. It is the spirits of these poor, unknown souls that are said to be responsible for the poltergeist activity that goes on in the library. Doors will open by themselves and then slam shut. Visitors report feeling invisible hands tap them on the shoulder or run through their hair. The ghost of Elizabeth Morgan, who was reburied in a marked grave on the property, is said to be seen walking the grounds of the library. Easton Public Library is located at 515 Church Street, Easton, Pennsylvania 18042.

STATE THEATRE CENTER FOR THE ARTS

The theatre was built in 1910 on the former site of the Northampton National Bank. The apparition of a man has been seen standing on the stage while the theatre is empty. Although many guests and employees have guessed at the identity of the ghost, confirmation came in the later years of the 1970s. A local historian witnessed the ghost *walking off the stage* one night. During later research, the historian identified the apparition he saw from a photograph he found. The man was J. Fred Osterstock, a manager of the theatre from 1936 to 1965. The theatre has embraced their spectral guest by adopting his name, Fred, for their annual "Freddy©" Awards, which honors extraordinary achievement in local high school theatre. State Theatre is located at 453 Northampton Street, Easton, Pennsylvania 18042. Website: http://www.statetheatre.org. *("Freddy©" is copyrighted by the State Theatre.)*

CONSTITUTION DRIVE

The ghosts of Constitution Drive come to us from a classic "ghost story" origin — a tragedy. It seems a train struck an unknown man who sustained a mortal injury to his leg. The man bled to death alongside the road. His ghost is seen walking along the road, walking two dogs of an unknown type. Strangely, the dogs are reported to have glowing, red eyes. What's interesting is that the dogs are not mentioned with the man's death. Constitution Drive is located between East Wyoming and Weil Streets, Allentown, Pennsylvania.

MORAVIAN COLLEGE

The apparition of a woman in a nurse's uniform has been seen wandering the halls of the old college. It is reported that a janitor witnessed another apparition in the basement. He saw a man with bandages around his head and one arm. The injured man walked around, oblivious of the janitor's attempts to see if he was ok. The injured man simply faded away, leaving the janitor confused and freaked out. In the Music Building, phantom footsteps are a common occurrence, as well as doors opening and closing on their own. The spirits of three men who allegedly hanged themselves haunt the basement of Rau Dormitory. Moravian College is located at 1200 Main Street, Bethlehem, Pennsylvania 18018.

THE SUN INN

This former hotel was restored as a museum and restaurant. A Lehigh Valley paranormal group has been investigating the site and apparently obtained a photograph of the ghost of Hughetta Bender, founder of the Sun Inn Preservation Association. The paranormal team has also captured numerous EVPs from several different entities, ranging from names being called out to a ghost that sings along when the piano is played. Sun Inn has been hosting public ghost hunts, available for a very reasonable price, and allows you to conduct your own investigation of the site. Sun Inn is located at 564 Main Street, Bethlehem, Pennsylvania 18018.

KEY THEATRE

The building dates back to 1914 when it was used as an auditorium. The stage area where the movie screen is was much wider than the current one. It later was used as a playhouse. There was some remodeling done in 1941. The original owner, when it became a theatre, was a man by the name of John Hersker. He was also the projectionist. An apparition, believed to be that of John Hersker, has been seen in the area just outside the doors, next to the concession stand. Several people have also witnessed a man standing on the stage, just to the right of the movie screen. This apparition, also believed to be John Hersker, seems to be watching the crowd as they enjoyed the movies. A shadow figure has been seen on the right side of the theatre, in the seating area. Behind the screen, several people have reported seeing "glowing, red eyes" that are only a few feet off the ground. During an investigation in June 2002, I was able to witness some of this activity myself, catching sight of a dark figure moving around the theatre seats on the right side of the room. Key Theatre is located at 29-31 West Broad Street, West Hazleton, Pennsylvania 18201. Phone: 570-455-2455.

AFTERWORD

A MATTER
OF RESPECT

DRIVING THE POINT HOME

Once you have finished reading this book, you'll have a few new sites to visit that may have paranormal activity... i.e. ghosts. For many of you, this may be an opportunity to check out new places to have an experience of your own. This is all well and good since this is how I started my ghost hunting adventures many years ago. My worn and weathered copy of *Ghosts of Berks County* still holds a special place in my library.

However, I must press upon you the fact that many (but not all) of these areas fall into two groups; the first group are the Private Residences, in which the owners were nice enough to share their story with us. In most cases, the identity of the owners and location of their homes have been kept confidential. This is to protect their families and privacy from the casual ghost hunter who may find the story interesting enough to pursue it. Honestly, I've done this in the past—I found out firsthand that privacy is paramount. So, if you do "figure out" where some of these places are, I would ask that you enjoy the story, enjoy the thrill of finding the site where the story took place...but *don't* disturb the owners (unless, of course, they want the publicity).

The second group involves cemeteries, which are easily accessible by everyone. Although there are usually signs posted, a small group of thrill seeking ghost hunters have chosen to ignore them. Cemeteries are *still* considered sacred ground, not playgrounds for ghost hunters. If there are signs posted, then obey the rules printed on them. These are not public grounds; the land is regulated property. You wouldn't break into a store after closing, would you? If the cemetery says it is closed at dusk, then you shouldn't be walking in at ten o'clock at night with your camera. The police will not accept your "Paranormal Investigator" badge as proof that you're allowed to be there.

Finally, *SHOW RESPECT* for the sites you visit.

Yeah, I know you've read this morality point a few times already in the course of reading this book. But, I don't think I can say it enough. We, as in ghost hunters, which include those of us who use the term "Paranormal Investigator," will always have to deal with the skeptics who love to go public (mostly for the attention they lack at home). By taking the extra steps to always watching each other's back, we'll slowly, but surely, turn the opinion the general public has of us.

Thank you, and good hunting...

MY SEMi-FiNAL WORD ON ORBS

I call this my "semi-final" word for a simple reason; no matter how many times I explain it and duplicate it, there will always be someone who will believe that their orb photo is different from everyone else's orb photograph. And because of this, I will never have the pleasure of a "final" word on the subject.

To some ghost hunters, the orb represents some type of spirit; be it a ghost, a demon, or simply an unknown form of energy dwelling in a dimension we have yet to discover through our current technology. Some will present hundreds upon hundreds of photographs, along with hours and hours of video...all with the intention of "proving" that orbs are spiritual beings from the other side of life.

For many years, I have been openly critical of images of orbs—and I will continue to be so. Since I consider myself an investigator of the paranormal, I feel it is my "duty" to thoroughly investigate the details of each case and phenomenon with every ounce of scientific knowledge I possess, or have at my disposal. In doing so, I have come to the conclusion that the phenomenon of the orb can be broken down to a simple explanation: *Orbs are a trick of light.*

There are many factors that contribute to the appearance of an orb on an image, be it a photograph or video, but the essential ingredient in every case is light. Without light, orbs would not show up on our photographs and video clips. Understand that I am not simply referring to the light from a camera flash (though this is the most common), but also light from spot lights, flashlights, and even our sun.

In the majority of orb images, the physical source of the orb comes in the form of dust particles, raindrops, and moisture (mist, fog, high humidity). The source will not appear beside, next to, above, or below the intended subject of the photograph, but within a few inches of the lens. It is within this "Orb Zone" that a dust particle or drop of moisture will appear completely out of focus, thus presenting an image both much larger than its original size and with a significant level of transparency. The "Orb Zone" is a product of something called Depth of Field.

Whenever your camera settles on a subject, it focuses on that distance to keep the subject in sharp focus. There is an area just before and just after that will appear in focus as well (though with a subtle difference). As objects appear farther away or closer to the camera, focus drops off. This is seen with a lot of portrait photography: the main subject is sharp, but the background is a blur of color. If you have ever used an SLR or DSLR camera and played with the manual focus, you know this effect well. Dust particles and raindrops too close to the camera lens will be extremely out of focus.

However, it is only with the addition of the camera flash that these anomalies become visible to us on the photograph. Why? In the case of dust particles, they are simply too small for us to notice as we normally see the world around us. Take the room you're in right now, look around — see any dust particles? Chances are, you don't. But wait for a sunny day (or now, if the sun is shining brightly) and look into the sunbeam that streams in through the window. Tiny particles will be seen floating around, flying straight across, doing loops, and even changing directions. Now look outside the beam of sunlight, the particles seem to disappear (much like orbs do in videos using night vision). The dust particles are all around you, but it takes a bright light to make them stand out.

In the case of moisture and rain, the causes are obvious and can easily be seen by the naked eye. The sad part is that many will choose to ignore the obvious, in light of an explanation to sustain their beliefs. Raindrops are highly reflective and will reflect the light of a camera flash quite easily — and from some distance. However, it is still those that are closest to the camera lens that will be out of focus, changing how they appear on a photograph. During a very light rain, or in a fog/misty area, each drop of moisture will reflect the light of a camera flash, giving you hundreds of orb images. Again, without the light of the flash, you would not see the image of an orb, unless...

Even though the flash from the camera is probably the brightest light source you'll have at the time the photograph is taken, we have to ask the question; What if the flash is not used? This is a good and fair question. A light source such as a flashlight, a spot light, or even a porch light can illuminate raindrops and dust particles enough for the camera to record their presence. However, in situations that would require a flashlight, the area would be too dark NOT to use a flash. However, a camera with the flash turned off would require a longer exposure in order to allow more light to enter the camera. This will usually negate any "orb" effect (a longer exposure will allow background light to replace the transparent image of the out-of-focus dust particle).

Let us not forget the "Daytime Orbs." It's these little anomalies that keep some die-hard believers on the front lines. However, there are several causes of these orbs that are indeed natural, rather than supernatural. The most common culprit is the sun. While taking photographs during the day, most tourists and ghost hunting photographers do not take into account the position of the sun and its interaction with the camera lens. An effect called Lens Flare occurs when sunlight comes into the view of the lens and causes the light to bounce between the lenses. It creates an orb-like image, and in some cases, several orbs in a row. The row of orbs can usually be traced straight back to the sun (also occurs with streetlights and other bright lights). Depending on the angle, the orb can have a slight oval shape to it, which is caused by the curve of the camera lens. In other cases, a hexagonal shape is produced. This is caused by the shape of the aperture of the camera reflecting back onto the lens.

The color of an orb has also been linked (without evidence) to the emotional state of the entity. In these cases, the orb image does not produce its own color, but will take on the colorcast of the light source. Keep in mind that a camera flash produces a bright, white light — giving white orbs. Standard bulbs (some spot lights, most porch lights) give off a yellow glow. These images are more common in photographs taken at night or inside a building or structure, where the lighting is not on par with the daytime sun. A darker background will make for a more noticeable orb. In addition, the transparency aspect of the out-of-focus dust particle/raindrop can take on a color tint of the object behind it, depending on how much (or how little) the orb suffered from the bleaching effect of the camera flash. A faint pink orb is usually the result of a dust particle caught in front of a red wall. Always look closely at the objects in your photographs, picking up on the subtle details of what's really there, instead of accepting it at face value.

Orbs will undoubtedly remain a topic of discussion, debate, and controversy, which in itself makes the orb a phenomenon. However, as I stated in the beginning of this section, I have always been openly critical of orb images — and I will continue to be so. What you have read here is only a small portion of the causes behind these images. Although there are many books out there that turn the study of orbs into a major project, they are simply filled with statements that contain many "ifs, perhaps, possibles, and mights." Don't get me wrong, I believe knowledge we obtain usually starts off as a theory. But the ideas, such as for the causes of the orb images, should be tested, experimented, and examined before presenting a conclusion, which should be backed by your work.

For me, I have duplicated the situations in the photographs and video brought to me by ghost hunters and investigators. I have reproduced the orb-effect just as the photographs and videos have presented. To this day, I have not seen an image of an orb that cannot be explained by simple, natural causes. One can argue about having feelings or having a reading at the same time, but the fact remains: dust particles, rain, snow, pollen, insects, reflections, and so on will easily explain the cause. Most commonly, dust particles will not cease to float in the air simply because someone has a "feeling." It just doesn't work that way. And taking photographs in the rain while looking for orbs is… just plain silly.

For more information, I'm going to include a shameless plug. Pick up a copy of *Orbs or Dust — A Practical Guide to False Positive Evidence* by yours truly. In this book, I go into much greater detail on how these, and other ghostly effects, are captured. There are dozens of experiments included, so you can duplicate the results yourself and get a better understanding of the natural causes behind many ghostly images.

GHOST HUNTING RESOURCE GUIDE

RESOURCE ONE:

LOCAL PARANORMAL GROUPS

Paranormal Investigators & Research Association
Founder: Kenneth Biddle
Email: Help@parainvestigator.org
Website: www.Parainvestigator.Org

Eastern Pennsylvania Paranormal Investigations
Founder: Greg Swatt
Email: Help@eppiteam.com
Website: www.eppiteam.com

Panther Valley Paranormal Society
Founder: Jerry Matika
Email: jerry@pvparanormal.com
Website: http://www.pvparanormal.com/

Berks Lehigh Paranormal Association
Founder: Rick Bugera
Email: Help@blpa.com
Website: www.blpa.com

PARA Pocono
Founder: Victoria
Website: http://www.para-help.com/index.html

Research and Investigate Paranormal Activity — R.I.P.A. LLC
Email: researchpara@yahoo.com
Website: http://ripa-online.ning.com/

ABE Paranormal
Founders: James and Carla Siegfried
Email: james@abeparanormal.com
Website: www.abeparanormal.com/index.html

Luzerne County Ghost Hunters
Email: contact-us@lcghosthunters.org
Website: www.lcghosthunters.org/index.html

RESOURCE TWO:

CEMETERY GUIDELINES

1. **Always seek out and obey the Rules of the cemetery you're exploring**. Although you may not see them right away, most cemeteries have a sign (or signs) posted listing the operating hours (usually sunrise to sunset) and rules for leaving items (usually flowers). If the sign states CLEARLY that the cemetery is closed after 7 p.m. and it's 7:15, you don't go in. It really is as simple as that. You see, if you get caught in there after hours, it's most likely that you'll get a ticket (or worse) for trespassing. When it comes out that you were in the cemetery "ghost hunting," it will end up making the rest of us look like idiots. Word will spread and before you know it, the local paper will run a story about vandalism, with a local resident blaming "those dang ghost hunters" for the damages (rather than the local kids). So...DO NOT TRESPASS!

2. **Take out whatever you bring in**. This means your trash, including water/soda bottles, battery wrappers, snack wrappers, used batteries, etc. Seriously, this should be common sense, but for some reason, it doesn't seem to be so common. In many cases, the upkeep for these old cemeteries is done by volunteers, not a paid staff. Just imagine putting in eight or nine hours of hard work on a Saturday or Sunday to make an area look nice and clear of junk...only to pass by that night and see a group of people casually toss aside a plastic wrapper from the fresh set of batteries they just put in their cameras. How would you feel? Whether you know or not, we ghost hunters have a reputation that effects us all, not just yourself. Many people see us as disrespectful, trying to stir up the dead, or just thrill seekers who care nothing for the graves we walk over. We need to show that we are respectful and we DO care about what we do and the places we visit. Remember, we are not simply protecting our own reputations, but those of ghost hunters everywhere.

3. **Leave what's in the cemetery, in the cemetery**...to a point. Basically, don't touch little trinkets you might find by headstones. Also, don't decide to take home any souvenirs. Flowers are a common sight at graves, but you'll also find areas where family and friends have left small items in remembrance. Leave them alone! The families of the person (or people) in the cemetery left them and they are a small but important way that the living can still connect with those who have passed. However, if you see a discarded wrapper or beer bottle, pick it up and put it in a trash can.

4. **Respect the Land**. A cemetery, by definition, is a place to bury our dead. It is not, by any means, to be considered a city dump. We've already covered that you should take out any trash you bring in, but do us all a favor and clean up any trash items you might find. It not only helps clean up the areas we investigate, but shows that "ghost hunters" care about what we do. I've turned a "quick trip" into several hours of hard work when I got the urge to clean up a forgotten cemetery (picking up trash, lifting headstones back up, putting signs back up).

5. **Respect the Property**. The headstones and monuments at cemeteries are placed there to honor and remember those that have passed away. The families of those who rest under the headstones and monuments have paid for them. They are not chairs, benches, canvases for bad artwork, or toys to knock down. If you see anyone desecrating the graves/monuments of cemeteries, notify the authorities. Many of us visit cemeteries so that we can feel a connection to those we lost. However, some of us use the cemeteries to look for ghosts (that are already restless). So do your part in making sure you, and the rest of us, will be able to continue to use cemeteries as investigation sites...by keeping the idiots out.

RESOURCE THREE:

CONDUCTING EVP SESSIONS

Courtesy of the PIRA website

Many ghost hunters just starting out believe that conducting an EVP session is simply pushing the "Record" button on an audio device and leaving it alone. They come back a few hours later, listen to the tape, and declare any voices or odd noises as EVPs. This really isn't the way it should be done, at least not if you want anyone to take you seriously. I've listed some guidelines below that my team and I follow in order to cut down on False Positive recordings. A "False Positive," as it pertains to paranormal activity, is any type of evidence (photograph, video, EVP, meter reading, etc.) that appears to be paranormal, but in reality, has a natural explanation.

Before we begin, I need to state that none of my team or I makes use of "White Noise." As far as we're concerned, this is counter-productive to our investigation. White Noise, by definition, is a type of noise that is produced by combining sounds of all different frequencies together. If you took all of the imaginable tones that a human can hear and combined them together, you would have what is called "White Noise." The adjective "white" is used to describe this type of noise because of the similar way White Light works. White Light is light that is made up of all of the different colors (frequencies) of light combined together (a prism or a rainbow separates white light back into its component colors). In the same way, White Noise is a combination of all of the different frequencies of sound. You can think of White Noise as 20,000 tones all playing at the same time. Because White Noise contains all frequencies, it is frequently used to mask other sounds. If you are in a hotel and voices from the room next-door are leaking into your room, you might turn on a fan to drown out the voices. The fan produces a good approximation of White Noise.

Why does that work? Why does White Noise drown out voices? Here is one way to think about it. Let's say two people are talking at the same time. Your brain can normally "pick out" one of the two voices and actually listen to it and understand it. If three people are talking simultaneously, your brain can probably still pick out one voice. However, if 1,000 people are talking simultaneously, there is no way that your brain can pick out one voice. It turns out that 1,000 people talking together sounds a lot like White Noise. So when you turn on a fan to create White Noise, you are essentially creating a source of 1,000 voices. The voice next-door makes it 1,001 voices, and your brain can't pick it out any more.

So, logically speaking, any EVP would be lost in the "crowd." There are many investigators who swear by the use of White Noise. However, there is no evidence that can definitively claim that this actually works better than simply using a recorder alone. We believe that adding White Noise allows the imagination to "create" voices within the recording rather than capturing a genuine EVP.

Now, onto how we conduct the session.

First and foremost, you need to establish a speaker. This person is the only one is allowed to speak while recording. Everyone else in the area should remain quiet. The reason for this is simple; having one known voice helps rule out other investigators as the source of "ghostly" voices.

The Speaker should establish that there is absolutely NO WHISPERING during the recordings. A large percentage of EVPs are recorded as a whispering voice, so it's imperative that none of the living whisper to each other. Keep in mind that if you can hear someone whisper, it's a sure thing that your recorder's microphone can "hear" it as well. However, even with such warnings, there are going to be a few ghost hunters who are convinced that they can whisper and get away with it. The Speaker should take this into account and announce all observed "whispering." Trust us; it'll be worth it later on when you're listening to the playback.

The Speaker is also in charge of announcing all outside noises, such as planes, cars, noises from equipment, and coughs and/ or sneezes from other investigators. Such announcements will help later on by identifying noises that may have otherwise been labeled "unknown." Some groups like to leave a recording device alone, allowing it to simply record whatever happens and review the findings later. There are many natural noises that are going to be recorded, but without a living person there to identify all of them when they happen, there can be a few that slip through. If a team member walks into the room and realizes there is a recording going on, they may decide to leave without disturbing the recorder. You won't get any ghostly voices, but you'll hear "ghostly" footsteps walking around!

Something else we'll throw in here: a recorder left alone can easily pick up the carried voices of ghost hunters who are walking around. Anything can happen; someone tells a joke in a lower floor and another person laughs or makes a response in a loud excited way. That sound can easily carry to the recorder, which may only pick up the louder voice…POOF, you've got an EVP. Air vents in a house or building can easily carry all sorts of noises. Who knows what you might pick up?

The Speaker now has one more job to do…ask the questions. The questions that are asked should depend on the situation. For the first time at a location, questions should be general interview types that cover a broad range. Since you really don't know who you might be talking to, this is the best way to gather some information. Any responses can be followed up during the next recording session. With some research of the site and any responses from the initial recording session, you'll be able to focus your questioning on more specific topics (For example specific names, dates, anniversaries, and events).

There will be times when someone in the group experiences something, and getting other investigator voices on the recording can't be helped. Although difficult, you have to keep track of who speaks. When you can, have the Speaker talk to the person who had the experience. The best-case scenario is that you'll only have two living voices on tape to account for. The worse case scenario is that everyone in the group will start talking and you''ll never know who's who.

When reviewing the recordings, listen closely. Noises can sound a bit differently when heard on playback. If you went ahead and left a recorder alone, you'll have your work cut out for you. If an EVP sounds like static, it probably is. Remember, just because the recording was made on a ghost hunt in a supposedly haunted location doesn't mean that every weird noise is an EVP. Our rule of thumb is simple: if we can hear the EVP clearly the first time then we've got something (real or not is yet to be determined). If we've got garbled noise or static, then we do not consider it an EVP.

RESOURCE FOUR:

GENERAL INVESTIGATION PROTOCOLS

Courtesy of the PIRA website

Every investigator, and every team, should design and follow a set of protocols. The reason being is that it shows a professional attitude towards this hobby. Protocols establish certain guidelines to keep procedures and evidence consistent throughout each investigation. Protocols can also keep you and your team members safe, as well as protect your equipment and evidence.

The following Protocols are a sample of the long list my PIRA team follows. Feel free to use them as they are or modify them to fit your needs. These are simply stepping stones; build with them as you see fit.

𝒲 Always get permission to be on a property. Whether you see "Posted" signs or not, chances are the land you're walking on (cemetery grounds) is private or semi-private property. Look for signs when you arrive, and when possible, get permission from the owners (or operators). Some places may be hesitant in allowing you to wander the grounds. My advice to you is this; be honest. Tell them why you're there and explain that you'd simply like to take photographs and a few recordings.

𝒲 We always carry proper ID. Proper ID is a license and/or some kind of picture identification.

𝒲 We always check out an area beforehand. This is either through a preliminary investigation or a simple walk-through at a cemetery. Getting the "Lay of the Land" can help by identifying hazards or problem areas. Taking reference photographs will give the rest of the team an idea of what to expect.

𝒲 We always treat the owners/operators and their property with respect, as if it were our own. We always conduct ourselves in a professional manner during the investigation. We want to be there and we want to come back, so we want to keep the clients happy!

❧ All equipment is checked three times. The first time is done prior to leaving for the investigation. The second check is when we arrive at the location. This means we have plenty of fresh or charged batteries on hand. Third time comes at the end of the investigation when we're cleaning up. Make sure you have everything!

❧ Camera straps are removed or wrapped tightly around the hand and/or wrist. Although I am aware of what a strap can do when it gets in front of the lens, I am also aware of how much some of these cameras cost. The possibility of dropping one's camera is very high, especially when we're walking around dark cemeteries or unfamiliar ground.

❧ Long hair is tied back or kept under a hat. Hair can easily be mistaken for a vortex or fast moving orb, so keep it out of the way.

❧ No perfumes or colognes. Perfume has been a classic ghostly event that many people claim to have experienced. In order to help keep any false positives out of the way, try to keep the perfumes/colognes off for the night.

❧ Photos and/or video taken in cold weather are done with our breathing in mind. We take steps to ensure we don't snap a nice picture of our frozen breath. Here's what we do: breathe in slowly and hold it for three to four seconds before snapping the picture. In all, this should give you an average of seven seconds for any "frozen breath" ("Ecto") to pass along.

❧ We do not conduct outside investigations during bad weather. This includes snow, rain, fog, and heat waves (too much dust). You've seen how these things can easily cause false positive images.

❧ Photographs are not taken indoors if there is an obvious problem with dust. If we can see it in the viewfinder, so can the camera. You can still snap photographs, but you'll have to discount all orb images.

❧ Camera lenses are cleaned only at the beginning of a new roll of film or disc. Spots on the lens can cause orb-like images.

If something gets on the lens afterward, you'll be able to compare its placement with other photos on the roll/disk to determine if its "lens dirt."

❦ Analog recorders must make use of an external microphone. This is to eliminate noise from the recorders internal gears. The little things are loud!

❦ Reflected surfaces are noted and avoided to the best of the investigator's ability. We all know that they sometimes just get in the picture anyway! So just keep note of where they are and if you think you caught a reflection.

❦ All teams should have no less than two investigators. This is for safety as well as having another person to witness an experience. It's the Buddy System!

❦ Evidence is not discussed with owners/operators until the team can evaluate it first. We don't want to jump the gun, so to speak. Go over your evidence thoroughly before coming to any conclusions.

❦ No Smoking. If the investigation is going to be exceptionally long or an overnighter, then a designated smoking area can be assigned. The investigation should break until at least ten minutes after the cigarette has been extinguished. This allows time for the smoke to totally dissipate.

❦ No Drugs or Alcohol is permitted before or during an investigation. This is just common sense. It compromises any experiences you may have, since we can easily blame it on the booze.

❦ During any private home investigation, we ask that only two people (the owners) be present. Any more than that can and will cause a disruption with our investigation. Ask that the owners not invite their friends over to watch the ghost hunters. This makes the whole investigation a waste of time.

❦ We do not take pictures of moving objects or from moving objects. This causes a blurring effect on everything and renders the photo useless.

Keep the fingers away from the lens. Index finger and thumb in "C" position with the rest tucked in.

The Most Important Guideline We Follow

We arrive with an open mind. We arrive with the idea that there may be something going on, but we also know that it could have a totally natural explanation. We will decide for ourselves, as should you. A Paranormal Investigator should not be trying to confirm a haunting or debunk one. We should be looking for the truth.

RESOURCE FIVE:

PIRA INVESTIGATION PROCEDURES

Courtesy of the PIRA website

Below you'll find a short description of the procedures we follow when on a case. These will give you an idea of how each step is done. You can take these basic ideas and expand on them, tweak them, or rearrange as you see fit. Just keep in mind that we've worked these out over the years and it seems to work really well for us.

1. Preliminary (Informal) Investigation
2. Group Evaluation
3. Full (Formal) Investigation
4. Evidence Review
5. Historical Research
6. Presentation of Evidence
7. Posting of Evidence
8. Follow-ups and Ongoing Investigations

PRELIMINARY INVESTIGATION

The first step in our investigation is done by a small (scouting) group, usually two to three members, to determine if a full investigation would be the best choice. Interviews, which may be videotaped (we recommend videotaping the interview), will be conducted with the owners, as well as any witnesses. Historical information is gathered as well as accounts of paranormal activity. Reference photos will be taken at this time to determine "hazard" areas (i.e. multiple reflective surfaces and mirrors, high EMF areas, drafty windows). The members will explain our equipment and usage, the procedures we'll be following, and answer any other questions presented to them. Being an informal investigation, it allows the investigators and owners to get to know each other before we come in with a big group of people and start wandering around their house or place of business. A deadline (excuse the pun) will be set to notify the owners if and when a full investigation will be scheduled. The preliminary investigation may last up to two hours.

GROUP EVALUATION

Step two is a meeting of all the members who would be participating in the investigation. Everyone will listen to the "Scouts'" description of the preliminary investigation, look at the reference photos, and hear the interviews. From there, we'll decide if a full investigation is needed. The owners will be notified either way. In the case that we do not see the need for a formal investigation, the reasons why will be explained in detail.

Those of us who went on the Preliminary investigation will not reveal any of the reported paranormal activity to the rest of the team. This is so that the rest of the team won't have any preconceived ideas on what and where activity is "supposed" to happen.

FULL INVESTIGATION

This will include as many members as can safely and efficiently do the investigation. A house is not a good place to shove in twenty investigators and the owners. The job just can't be done right. So the number of members will reflect the amount of space that needs to be covered. This may include having a joint investigation with another paranormal group if the place is rather large. Investigators will break up into teams and cover as much area as time permits. Investigators will document any and all experiences during the investigation for review and comparison later. During this time investigators will use various pieces of equipment in all areas that we are permitted.

EVIDENCE REVIEW

After all is said and done, we really get down to work. Don't be alarmed, but this step may take a little time. All of the evidence collected (photographs, audio, video, personal experiences, etc.) now has to be reviewed. This means that if we took two hours of video, then we need to sit and watch two hours of video. This doesn't include stopping, rewinding, and watching again in slow motion to be certain if we saw something. Basically, a two-hour video can turn into two or three hours of viewing. Audio recordings are the same deal. Pictures sometimes need a few days for developing. All of that and our day jobs!? Always be prepared to spend a lot of time going

HISTORICAL RESEARCH

With a site that is truly haunted, we believe historical research is the key to finding out the "who, what, when, where, how and why" behind the activity. This step may use a few or all of our members and can last anywhere from a few hours to a few days. It all depends on the site. We've had places in which a ton of history was found in one sitting of three hours and others that have taken two teams and two days at two locations (whew!) to gather all the information available.

PRESENTATION OF EVIDENCE

All of the evidence — the good as well as the bad — will be presented to the owners. At this time, we'll go over any experiences we may have had and go over any positive evidence. We'll also go over any natural explanations we may have found.

Before we're done, we'll discuss any restrictions that the owners may have concerning the posting of the evidence to the website. We will also determine if the history of the property should be researched to identify possible causes of the activity. This means, simply, that we find out who the ghosts are.

POSTING OF EVIDENCE

All evidence, good and bad, may be posted to the website. The restrictions set forth by the owners will be honored. Written accounts will be posted in an entertainment format, with full reports kept on file at PIRA's office. The best pictures of positive and negative results will be posted. Audio will be posted if we get a clear, understandable EVP. Videos will be stored at PIRA's office and will not be posted, unless it contains a very interesting bit of footage.

FOLLOW-UPS AND ONGOING INVESTIGATIONS

This last step may not always happen. If we find that all of the reported activity has legitimate, natural explanations — and we found absolutely no evidence to support paranormal activity — then a follow-up would be a waste of time and money for our team.

However, there will be sites that present some definite positive results. Our first order of business will be to attempt to recreate and duplicate those positive results. This is when we'll conduct several Follow-up investigations. If we cannot duplicate the results and everything else checks out okay, then we believe we may have a truly active site.

An active site, if the owners agree, warrants an ongoing investigation. To us, this means a visit to the site at least once a year. If time and scheduling allow, we'll visit a lot more than that.

BiBLiOGRAPHY & RESOURCES

Adams III, Charles J. *Ghost Stories of Berks County.* Reading, Pennsylvania: Exeter House Books, 1982

Adams III, Charles J. and Seibold, David J. *Ghost Stories of the Lehigh Valley.* Reading, Pennsylvania: Exeter House Books, 1993.

Hauck, Dennis W. *The National Directory of Haunted Places.* New York, New York: Penduin Books 1994.

Stefko, Jill. "Haunted Easton, PA Library." Article for Suite101.com: 2007

PERSONAL INTERVIEWS & CORRESPONDENCE

Taylor, Kristina
   Personal Interview. *The Wydnor Hall Inn.* 2007

Torend, Frederick
   Personal Interview. *The Lady in the Blue Dress.* 2008

Gruber, Rick
   Personal Interview. *The White Palm Tavern.* 2009

White Palm Tavern Employees
   Personal Interview. *The White Palm Tavern.* 2009

Diane
   Personal Interview on the side of the road. *Bruce the Bum.* 2008

Victoria
   Personal Interview. *The Lake House Hotel.* 2009

Joe & Maria
   Personal Interview. *The "Haunted" Cemetery.* 2000

Bob Radle
   Personal Interview. *The Freemansburg Cemetery*. 2001
   Email conversations. *The House of the Hanging Man*. 2008

Former Owner of Residence
   Personal Interview. *A Loved One's Visit*. 2002

Kissiner, James
   Email Conversation, Personal Interview. *The Ghost of the Kilns*.
   2008

WEBSITE RESOURCES

http://lehighvalleyhistory.net/

http://www.lehighcounty.org/Hist/hist.cfm?doc=hist_home.htm

http://www.lvrrhs.org/history/index.htm

http://www.leo.lehigh.edu/envirosci/enviroissue/sprawl/LVhistory.html

http://www.associatedcontent.com/article/628813/haunted_places_in_the_
lehigh_valley.html?cat=16

http://www.statetheatre.org/

http://www.abeparanormal.com/localhaunts.html

http://home.comcast.net/~parainvestigator/Index/Main.html

http://www.pvparanormal.com/

http://www.whitepalmtavern.com/

http://www.uandwecemetery.org/

http://www.newhotelofhorror.com/home.html

http://www.associatedcontent.com/article/393277/charming_haunted_
allentown_pennsylvania.html?cat=8

http://www.ghostsofamerica.com/1/Pennsylvania_Allentown_ghost_sightings.html

http://home.comcast.net/~parainvestigator/Reports/Key.html

http://cinematreasures.org/theater/12623/

INDEX

"A Dark Figure Steps Towards Him" — A former member has a close encounter with a Shadow Person.

"An EVP Experiment" — A controlled test for EVP turns up an interesting result

Bethlehem Hotel, The, Page 129
437 Main Street,
Bethlehem, Pennsylvania

"Strange Shadows" — Shadows, apparitions and voices are experienced in this old hotel.

Cedar Crest College, Page 128
100 College Drive,
Allentown, Pennsylvania

"Wanda" — A ghostly woman has been seen in the halls.

Constitution Drive, Page 130
Between East Wyoming Street and Weil Street
Allentown, Pennsylvania

"A Tragedy" — A train accident leads to the ghost of a man and two dogs roaming this road for all of eternity.

Easton Public Library, The, Page 129
515 Church Street,
Easton, Pennsylvania

"Over Five Hundred Graves" — Many graves were uncovered during construction, and it seems that some of the souls are still restless.

Freemansburg Cemetery, Page 98
Intersection of Monroe Street and Walnut Street,
Freemansburg, Pennsylvania

"The Boy with the Bright, Red Hair" – An unknown boy has been seen playing around the large tree in the center of the cemetery.

**Lake House Hotel, Page 61
Route 115 and Cherry Valley Road,
Saylorsburg, Pennsylvania**

"The Man in the Window" — While snapping photos of the front porch, the image of a bearded man could be seen looking out the window. The photographer could not duplicate the results.

"The Guy in a Hoodie" — Staff members have seen a young man wearing a hooded sweatshirt walking from room to room.

"Footsteps are another common occurrence" — Witnesses are amazed as they hear footsteps come down the stairs, but unable to see the entity causing them.

"The Shadow Man" — A tall, dark figure was witnessed in the basement.

"The Ringing Telephone" — Stories tell of an old telephone prop that rings, even though it's not a working phone.

"The Shadow Man, Part 2" — An earlier sighting gets confirmation from an entire group of ghost hunters.

"Nancy" — Using several microphones and sensitive recording equipment, a trapped spirit is able to tell us her name.

**Moravian College, Page 130
1200 Main Street,
Bethlehem, Pennsylvania**

"Apparitions" — A phantom nurse and injured man have been reported in the halls and basement.

**Muhlenberg College, Page 129
2400 Chew Street,
Allentown, Pennsylvania**

"Oscar Bernheim" — The former owner is believed to walk the grounds.

State Theatre Center for the Arts, Page 130
453 Northampton Street,
Easton, Pennsylvania

"J. Fred Osterstock" — The apparition of a former manager has been witnessed by staff and guests.

Sun Inn, The, Page 131
564 Main Street,
Bethlehem, Pennsylvania

"Ghostly Photograph" — A paranormal team believes they have captured the image of the Founder of the Preservation Association.

Union and West End Cemetery, Page 31
North 10th Street, between West Pine and West Gordon Streets,
Allentown, Pennsylvania

"Lady in the Blue Dress" — An old woman in a light blue dress is seen cleaning up the cemetery after a storm.

White Palm Tavern, Page 47
5 Centre Avenue,
Topton, Pennsylvania

"Emma" — The ghost of a little girl has been seen by many guests as she walks through the Dining Room.

"The Priest" — The ghost of this clergyman has a deep dislike for holidays, especially Christmas.

"The Gardener" — An elderly man still tends to a garden that has long been replaced by a concrete patio.

"Strange Scents" — The scent of Sulfur has been reported by staff coming from the basement.

"Servers Report Being tripped…" — Waitresses report being tripped while carrying trays.

"Electrical Problems" — Since the BLPA began investigating, the site has had a dramatic increase in electrical issues.

"The Robin-Egg Blue Dress" — Investigator Rick Bugera witnessed an apparition of a woman as he sat with the owner.

"Stoppage of Time" — While heading up the stairs, a former resident experiences a stop in the flow of time, as well as a ghost with a fuzzy face.

"Footsteps to the Basement" — While this author and another investigator were in the basement, phantom footsteps walked up to the doorway.

"Falling Cookbooks" — Books that are snuggly placed between others have been found on the floor when the owner opens up in the morning.

Wydnor Hall Inn, Page 14
3612 Old Philadelphia Pike,
Bethlehem, Pennsylvania

"The Little Girl" — The spirit of a little who drowned in a nearby creek, is seen running down the hall into the kitchen.

"Face in the Doorway" — The owner has sighted a man's face in the doorway, watching her as she cleans the rooms of the second floor.

"Pipe Smoking Ghost" — The ghost of a man in a tweed jacket has been witnessed smoking a pipe in the Common room.